LIAM MAGUIRE'S

Hockey Trivia   Book I

Best of luck with the Thunder
next year.

Liam
Maguire

Foreword by Dick Irvin

Published by

GENERAL STORE
PUBLISHING HOUSE

1 Main Street, Burnstown, Ontario, Canada K0J 1G0
Telephone (613) 432-7697 or (613) 432-9385

ISBN 0-919431-88-7
Printed and Bound in Canada.

Layout and Design by Mervin Price
Cover Design by Leanne Enright

General Store Publishing House gratefully acknowledges the assistance
of the Ontario Arts Council.

Canadian Cataloguing in Publication Data

Maguire, Liam
    Liam Maguire's Hockey trivia

ISBN 0-919431-88-7

    1. Hockey — Miscellanea. 2. National Hockey
League — Miscellanea.   I. title.   Title: Hockey trivia.

GV847.M455   796.962   C94-900332-8

Cover Photo: Hockey Hall Of Fame

First Printing April 1994

DEDICATION

To my parents, Pat and Sarah, to whom I owe everything;
To my fiancé, and soon-to-be wife, Liz Heney, with whom
I want to do everything;
and
to my brothers, Mike and Sean, who as brothers go,
are two of my best friends in the world.

ACKNOWLEDGMENTS

No book, no matter how big or how small, gets done without a lot of people's help. In this case, before there can be a book there had to be the knowledge and the where-with-all to use it. During the formative teenage years, two good friends were responsible for piquing my interest in hockey beyond being just a fan: Phil Byrne and Brian Leroux. By my early twenties, I had met Jeff Dilabio. A friend to this day and back then every bit a trivia guru. Radio station CFRA started me professionally. The late Ernie Calcutt, Hal Anthony and Lowell Green were instrumental in my early beginnings on radio. Randy Tieman of CFCF brought me to Montreal and introduced me to Dick Irvin. To both of them, especially Mr Irvin, I owe a great deal of thanks.

Two men in Toronto, although neither from there originally, never stopped offering me encouragement to write and strive to be better! Chuck "Spider" Jones and my Uncle John Payne. Along the whole way were my friends, who somehow put up with my endless barrage of stats, names and numbers mixed in with the odd pint. Guys like the Headers, Tom Bissonnette and Kevin Jardine, Oli, Gordo, Paul Rushleau, Conan, Sammy, Bizard, Doyley, Howser, Smurph, Kenny Craig, Fluff, Gloves (all of them), Smitty, the Boog-a-loo, Hammer, Johnny Mott, Norton Malarka, Browner, R.B. Rory Bradley, Checker and every lad from the Valley I've ever tipped one back with. Thanks has to go to my brothers Mike and Sean for putting up with me in the mid to late seventies when I was reading thirty to forty hours a week and no doubt driving them crazy. And now I'm doing it again, only this time with the love of my life, Liz Heney; thanks sweetheart.

To Yvan Cournoyer, my all time hero, who I now can call a friend. Thanks to Ron Maclean and Ralphie, and for their endorsements. A big thank you to the people responsible for what you have in your hands now; Tim Gordon, Rosemary Nugent, Leanne Enright, Mervin Price and the rest of the staff at General Store Publishing House. To Dad, Sah and Kathryn Paquette for their tireless work on the computer, correcting errors, and inputing new material. To all the people who supplied me with questions over the years: guys like Ron Francis, Paul Petrocco, Mike Bolton, Dave Gross, Kevin Daly, Andrew Marquis, Dan Seguin, Brian Smith, Gerry Rochon, Mark Freer and to many others to mention. And finally to everybody who has called or written from Stoneham, Quebec to Dublin Ireland, from Cornerbrook, NFLD to Vancouver BC,

Thank you, thank you, thank you.

Liam Patrick Maguire

INTRODUCTION

It seems like hockey has been a part of my life forever. By the time I was ten, I was accumulating and storing statistics. By sixteen, the passion had turned into an obsession – studying, memorizing, reading and researching. The crowning glory of my youth took place on May 21, 1981, a day before my twenty-second birthday, when I was a guest on the Hal Anthony talk show on radio station CFRA in Ottawa. In the two hours that I was on the air, my destiny changed forever. I was now the unofficial hockey trivia expert and the snowball had begun to roll down the hill. In the thirteen years since that debut, I've made over 500 appearances on radio, television, banquets and dinners and it is from these appearances that the formation of the book was born. The personalities that I have met, players, media and fans have provided me with questions, stories and anecdotes; some of which I'm sure you have never heard.

This is more than a book of numbers or names. A lot of attention has been paid to details that enhance the original question. There are only 243 base questions, however they are backed up with over 500 additional facts or pieces of information. This is a hockey fans dream no matter what level of fan you might be. Sit back, snap a cap and enjoy.

Liam Maguire

FOREWORD

At various times during the 1960's and 70's I was the host of a television program entitled "Know Your Sports". This gave me some notoriety as an "expert" in sports trivia, which is easy when you have the answers in your hand during the show. But the image stuck and, from time to time, people would try to stump me, especially with questions about hockey.

In the early 1980's, one of my co-workers at CFCF-TV in Montreal came into my office, introduced me to a young man from Ottawa, Liam Maguire, and dared me to stump him with a hockey question. This wasn't a new experience for me, so I tossed off a question of medium difficulty, which Liam answered immediately. In the next few minutes, I unloaded my heavy artillery, and Liam had the answer to every one, usually embellishing his answer with extra information about the incident, game or player involved. I was very impressed.

Over the next few years, Liam Maguire appeared on my TV show, "Hockey Magazine", a total of fourteen times; it was always the same routine. I would prepare a list of thirty questions and ask them in rapid fire fashion. If I could catch Liam on two or three per show, I figured I had a good day. The viewers loved it.

Liam and I often discussed the possibility of him putting his vast knowledge of hockey into a book. Now, I am glad to see it has happened. So read and enjoy. You'll not only learn how many questions, and answers, he can come up with, you'll learn a lot about hockey history too. And don't feel bad when Liam keeps stumping you for the answers. He's been doing it to me for years.

by Dick Irvin

TABLE OF CONTENTS

THE NUMBER GAME

Sweater numbers have long been a part of hockey trivia. In 1912, the Patrick brothers, Lester and Frank, started their own league on the West Coast called the Pacific Coast Hockey League. The PCHL soon rivalled the number one league in the East, the National Hockey Association (NHA). One of the many innovations the Patricks were responsible for, was putting numbers on the back of sweaters to better identify the players. By 1918, the NHA had given way to the NHL and the hierarchy of the new league followed the Patricks' lead, numbering the sweaters. The practice took an interesting turn in the Thirties when some of the teams gave out high football type numbers hoping to cash in on the success the NFL was having with high numbers. Most notable were the Montreal Canadiens, who employed three number 99s during the 1934-35 season: Leo Bourgeault, Des Roche and Joe Lamb.

1) The Boston Bruins lead the way in the NHL with seven sweater numbers retired. What numbers are they and who wore them?

a) 2- Eddie Shore
    3- Lionel Hitchman
    4- Bobby Orr
    5- Aubrey "Dit" Clapper
    7- Phil Esposito
    9- Johnny Bucyk
    15- Milt Schmidt

Eddie Shore and Bobby Orr are documented later in the book. Most people are aware of Phil Esposito and Johnny Bucyk's accomplishments. Milt Schmidt was a member of the famous "Kraut Line", which became known as the "Kitchener Kids" when they rejoined the league after the

Second World War. Lionel Hitchman was a defenceman who won the Cup, originally with the Ottawa Senators and then joined the Bruins in their first season of 1924-25. He played on their first Cup winning team in 1929. "Dit" Clapper was the first 20 year man in the NHL and was the first man to be on the official All-Star team in two different positions. He was on the second team as a right winger in 1931 and 1935. He was a first team defenceman in 1939, 1940 and 1941 and finally a second team defenceman in 1944.

2) Who were the first players to wear number 13 in the NHL?

a) Bill Boucher of the Montreal Canadiens in 1922-23, Harold Hart of the Detroit Red Wings in 1927 and Jack Stoddard of the New York Rangers in 1952 and 1953.

3) What member of the Kansas City Scouts wore number 13 in the club's first two years?

a) Robin Burns. He came over from the Penguin organization where he wore three numbers: 10, 20 and 25. With Kansas City, he thought he'd be different.

4) Besides the three Montreal Canadiens in 1934-35 and Wayne Gretzky, who were the other two players to wear 99?

a) Wilf Paiement with the Toronto Maple Leafs from 1979/80-1981/82 and Rick Dudley with the Winnipeg Jets, in 1981.

5) What two NHL players have worn number 0?

a) Paul Bibeault, a goaltender with the Montreal Canadiens in 1942-43, and Neil Sheehy, of the Hartford Whalers, in 1988.

6) What goaltender wore number 00 and why?

a) John Davidson of the New York Rangers. After Phil Esposito and Ken Hodge both began wearing 77 and 88 respectively, Esposito tried to coerce the entire team into wearing double digits, even the goalies. Davidson eventually went back to number 30.

7) Only one other Montreal Canadien ever wore the number 7, made famous by Howie Morenz. Who was he, and what other distinctions did he have?

a) Ogilvie Cleghorn, better known as Odie to his friends, was part of the first brother combination to play for the Montreal Canadiens in the NHL. His brother's name was Sprague. Odie first wore number 6, then took 7 and, after the arrival of Morenz, he went back to 6. He was also the first coach of the expansion Pittsburgh Pirates Hockey Club in the 1925-26 hockey season, and he even played goaltender one game when regular Roy Worters was hurt. On top of that, he is credited with being the first coach to change his lines on the fly.

8) There are four number 8s retired in the NHL. Who are they?

a) Bill Goldsworthy   –   Minnesota North Stars
   Marc Tardif   –   Quebec Nordiques
   Barclay Player   –   St Louis Blues
   Frank Finnigan   –   Ottawa Senators

9) Match the player with his first number in the NHL.

   Gordie Howe   15
   Bobby Hull   17
   Maurice Richard   16

a) Howe first wore 17 and then switched to 9 to get a lower berth on the trains because the lower berths were bigger. Richard first wore 15 and switched in honour of his first born; a daughter that weighed nine pounds. Hull first wore 16, and then 7, before he settled in with the number 9. The players who wore number 9 before each of these players were Roy Conacher before Howe on Detroit, Charlie Sands before Richard on Montreal and Bronco Horvath before Hull on Chicago.

10) Who wore number 10 on the Montreal Canadiens before Guy Lafleur?

a) Frank Mahovlich for one game. After his trade to the Habs on January 13, 1971, number 27 was not readily available so he took 10. Bill Collins, who had been wearing it, was involved in the trade for the Big M. The one game was against the Minnesota North Stars, January 14th and the score was 3-3.

11) The goal that cost Don Cherry his job with the Boston Bruins was scored on May 10, 1979, at the Montreal Forum by number 11 of the Canadiens. Who was he?.

a) Yvon Lambert of the Habs scored in overtime at the 9:33 mark in Game Seven of the semi-finals to sink the Bruins and Don Cherry. Grapes was at the end of the line with GM Harry Sinden and the only thing that might have saved his job was a victory over the Canadiens and a berth in the finals.

12) The only member of the Montreal Canadiens to score five goals or more in a game during the 1970s wore number 12. Who was he?

a) Yvan Cournoyer on February 15, 1975, scored five against Chicago and goalie Mike Veisor in a 12-3 Montreal win.

13) What numbers did Bobby Orr wear with the Bruins before 4 and who wore 4 before Orr?

a) Orr was assigned numbers 30 and 27 in training camp. Defenceman Albert "Junior" Langois was wearing number 4 but was injured in training camp. Orr had worn 2 in Junior and 4 was as close as he would get to it so he took it.

14) Only two lines in NHL history have been nicknamed because of their sweater numbers. What were the nicknames and who were the players?

Still in his teens, Bobby lines up with the veterans of the Boston Bruins in his first practice.

a) "The Dice Line" - Calgary Flames, 1980s. Colin Patterson, Rich Kromm and Carey Wilson all wore double number digits – 11, 22 and 33 respectively– hence the name.

"The Crazy Eights" - Philadelphia Flyers, 1992-93. Eric Lindros, Mark Recci and Brent Fedyck wore 88, 8 and 18, respectively.

15) This former Toronto Maple Leaf player wore number 27 and later went on to coach the team. Who was he?

a) Mike Nykoluk who played 32 games with the Leafs in 1957 and then coached them from 1981-1984.

16) What two players have had their sweaters retired with two different teams?

a) Gordie Howe-number 9 with Detroit and Hartford. Bobby Hull-number 9 with Chicago and Winnipeg.

17) Irvine "Ace" Bailey of the Toronto Maple Leafs wore number 6, which was retired for him. The Leafs brought it out of retirement for which player and what numbers had he worn previously?

a) Ron Ellis wore numbers 11 and 8 when the Leafs decided to give him Bailey's number 6 during the 1964-65 season.

18) What number did Bobby Hull wear with the Hartford Whalers in 1979-80?

a) He wore number 16. His longtime sweater number 9 was taken by Gordie Howe so Hull opted for the number which he first wore with Chicago in 1957-1958.

19) The only other number besides 8 retired on Minnesota is 19. He is the only player in the NHL to die as a result of an on-ice injury. Who was he and what two players checked him causing him to hit his head on the ice?

a) Bill Masterson was 29 years old when he was upended after a collision with Ron Harris and Larry Cahan of the Oakland Seals on January 13, 1968. Thirty hours later he was dead from head injuries. He was not wearing a helmet.

20) What Russian hockey player made number 20 famous to all Canadians who grew up in the 1970s and early 1980s?

a) Vladislav Tretiak, of the Russian Red Army team and the National and Olympic team, wore number 20 throughout his international career.

21) This former number 88 in the NHL has the distinction of scoring the first penalty shot goal in New Jersey Devil history, and he has a famous brother with six Stanley Cup rings. Who is he?

a) Rocky Trottier, Bryan's brother, wore number 88 with the Devils during his brief stay with them. On February 17, 1984, he scored their first penalty shot goal against Andy Moog of the Edmonton Oilers.

22) This player is the only Pittsburgh Penguin to have his sweater retired and was also the first Penguin to score an overtime goal. Who was he?

a) Michel Brière, their second selection in the 1969 amateur draft, wore number 21. He scored the deciding goal in the first playoff series the Penguins played in 1970. It was a four game sweep over Oakland. Brière scored in overtime in the fourth game. He died that May as a result of injuries in a car accident.

23) Only two players have had their sweaters retired by teams they had never played for in the NHL. Who are they?

a) J. C. Tremblay's number 3, with the Quebec Nordiques, and Johnny McKenzie's number 19, with the Hartford Whalers. Both players were rewarded with the honour because of their play with those teams in the World Hockey Association (WHA). Frank Finnigan's number 8 with the Ottawa Senators would not count on the technicality that he did indeed play for Ottawa, however that was in the 1920s and 30s before they folded.

24) The first number retired by the Vancouver Canucks belonged to a player who also had the first two goal game in Canuck history when they recorded their first franchise win, a 5-3 victory over the Toronto Maple Leafs. Who is the player?

a) Wayne Maki, who wore number 11. He died of a brain haemorrhage in 1973. Stan Smyl's number 12 also retired.

25) What Czechoslovakian forward wore number 66 during the 1982-83 season?

a) Milan Novy of the Washington Capitals.

26) Who wore number 27 for Toronto before Darryl Sittler?

a) Tough one here. A defenceman by the name of Gord Nelson for three games during the 1969-70 season.

27) What numbers did Phil Esposito wear with the Rangers before he took 77?

a) Numbers 12 and 5.

28) Who wore number 7 on Boston after Phil Esposito?

a) A left winger by the name of Sean Shanahan, who played only six games with Boston in 1977-78 after signing as a free agent. He was actually booed for wearing the sweater.

29) What goaltender played the least number of games in their NHL career of any Bill Jennings trophy winner?

a) Darren Jensen of the Philadelphia Flyers played one game in 1985, and then 29 games in 1986, where he shared the Jennings Trophy with Bob Froese. Ron Hextall appeared on the scene the next year and Jensen retired with a total of thirty games played in his career.

30) What Vézina winning goaltender played the fewest games in his career?

a) Johnny Mowers of Detroit played 152 games from 1941 to 1947 and won the Vézina in 1943. Pelle Lindberg played 157 games from the 1981-1982 season until his death on November 10, 1985. He had just won the Vézina Trophy in 1985.

TRADES AND TRANSACTIONS

Trades have been an important part of hockey even prior to the NHL. One of the first on record was a deal in 1913, which saw the Montreal Canadiens receive Newsy Lalonde from the Vancouver Millionaires. The transaction was finally completed the following year in 1914, when Vancouver received Didier Pitre to complete the exchange. This chapter will deal with some of the bigger deals, some of the best and some of the worst.

1) The first three team deal in the history of the NHL involved two of the biggest names in the game. What were the details?

a) Most hard core hockey fans are aware that Howie Morenz played for two other teams in the NHL besides the Canadiens. However, they probably do not know the deals that got him there. On September 22, 1934, Howie Morenz was traded from the Habs, along with Marty Burke and goaltender Lorne Chabot, to Chicago for Lionel Conacher, Roger Jenkins and Leroy Goldsworthy. The Habs then traded Conacher and the rights to a player, named Herb Cain, to the Montreal Maroons for Nels Crutchfield. Just to let you know who we're talking about here, Morenz's story is well documented

Superstar Howie Morenz shown here in a Chicago uniform.

and it's covered in a later chapter. Roger Jenkins is the only number 88 in Montreal history, Leroy Goldsworthy wore 75. Lionel Conacher was voted Canada's athlete of the half century in 1950, and Herb Cain, after making his way to the Boston Bruins, won the scoring championship in 1944 with what was then a record 82 points. Morenz was later dealt from Chicago to the Rangers, in January of 1936, for Glen Brydson, before finally making his way back to his beloved Canadiens for the start of the following season, 1936-37.

2) What was the famous three-way deal in 1971 involving Bernie Parent?

a) On February 1, 1971, the Flyers orchestrated a three-way deal involving Toronto and Boston. The Flyers traded Bernie Parent and a second-round pick to Toronto for Bruce Gamble, Mike Walton and a first-round pick. The Flyers then traded Walton to Boston for Rick Macleish and Danny Schock. What confuses people about this, is the fact that they remember Parent with Philadelphia when they won their Stanley Cups in 1974 and '75. What happened was, two years later, Toronto returned Parent to the Flyers with a second-round pick for a first-round pick and goalie Doug Favell. Follow all that? Good.

3) The winner of the scoring championship in 1946 and 1947 was traded on November 2, 1947, in a seven player block-buster deal. Who was involved?

a) Max Bentley of the Chicago Blackhawks was a superstar of his era when he was dealt to the Leafs. Accompanying him was a minor league player named Cy Thomas, who would play only fourteen games in his NHL career. He was also born in Wales. Going to Chicago from Toronto was an entire line, known in those days as the "Flying Forts" because they were all from Fort William, Ontario. Gus Bodnar, Gaye Stewart and Norman "Bud" Poile were the forwards; Bob Goldham and Ernie Dickens were the two defencemen. The trade gave Toronto unprecedented strength down the middle with Bentley, Syl Apps and Ted Kennedy. It was the biggest deal of the 1940s.

4) On August 20, 1951, six players were traded from Detroit to Chicago for a minor league player and $75,000. Who was involved?

a) Chicago Black Hawks were in the middle of a losing streak that would see them finish last in the NHL, nine out of eleven seasons. This deal was part of a grand scheme by the league to help the Hawks. Even though $75,000 was a large sum of money in 1951, it still was a bargain for what Chicago got: Clare Martin, Jim Peters, Max McNab, Clare "Rags" Raglan, George Gee and Jim McFadden for Hugh Coflin and the money. Martin was with the Red Wings when they won the Stanley Cup in 1950. Jim Peters won three Cups: one in Montreal in 1946, the Detroit victory in 1950 and a third with Detroit again in 1954. Max McNab would later become GM of the Washington Capitals and, after that, the New Jersey Devils. He also had a son who played in the NHL (Peter) . Rags Raglan has a son who is playing right now, Herb Raglan. George Gee assisted on the last two goals scored by Bill Mosienko the night he fired three in 21 seconds. Jim McFadden was a former Calder Trophy winner with Detroit in 1948. Born in Belfast, Northern Ireland, McFadden has the distinction of being the second oldest player to win the rookie award at 28 years of age. The minor league player, Hugh Coflin, played a total of 31 games in his NHL career.

5) What Hall of Fame player was traded back twice to his original team?

a) Goaltender Terry Sawchuk was originally a Detroit Red Wing. He was traded to Boston in a nine player deal and then back to Detroit for Johnny Bucyk. Later he was claimed by Toronto in the waiver draft and then by Los Angeles in the expansion draft before being traded back to Detroit again. On that occasion, he was dealt for the son of a man he once played with, Jimmy Peters Jr. In one final deal, Detroit sent him to the Rangers where he played his final season in 1969-70. He suffered an untimely death that summer.

6) Phil Esposito was in two huge deals 8 1/2 years apart. Who else was involved?

a) On May 15, 1967, Phil Esposito, Ken Hodge and Fred Stanfield were traded from Chicago to Boston for Gilles Marotte, Jack Norris and Hubert "Pit" Martin. The three ex-Hawks would be instrumental in helping the Bruins win two Cups in 1970 and 1972. On November 7, 1975, Esposito was dealt to the New York Rangers along with Carol Vadnais for Jean Ratelle, Brad Park and Joe Zanussi. Neither team won the Cup but both enjoyed success.

7) Frank Mahovlich was also in one big transaction and another semi-big deal in his career. Who were the players in those trades?

a) On March 3, 1968, the man known as the Big M got out from under Punch Imlach's thumb and was dealt to the Detroit Red Wings from the Toronto Maple Leafs. Along with the Big M were Pete Stemkowski, Garry Unger and the rights to Carl Brewer, who had been re-instated as an amateur. Going from Detroit were Norm Ullman, Floyd Smith and Paul Henderson, who four years later would score the goal heard around the world.

Mahovlich's second deal saw him go to the Habs alone for three players: Mickey Redmond, Guy Charron and Bill Collins. The deal took place January 13, 1971. That year in the playoffs, Mahovlich helped Montreal to one of the biggest upsets in NHL history as the Habs upended the Bruins in a seven game series in the quarter-finals. He recorded 27 points in those playoffs which tied a record set only the year before by Phil Esposito.

8) How did Montreal acquire the first overall pick to draft Guy Lafleur in 1971?

a) This is actually a two part answer. Part one took place a full year before Lafleur's draft year. On May 22, 1970, the Canadiens traded Ernie Hicke and their first round pick from that season to the Oakland Seals for a player named Francois Lacombe and the Seals' first pick the following year,

Lafleur's draft year. Now they had the pick, but they needed the Seals to finish last. Ordinarily not a problem, however with Hicke's contribution, Oakland (known at this point as the California Golden Seals) actually climbed out of the basement at one point and were in a race with the LA Kings for last. Master trader Sam Pollock, GM of the Canadiens, traded Ralph Backstrom to LA for Gord Labossiere and Ray Fortin. Backstrom's experience, and his 27 points in 33 games, helped push LA to within five games of a .500 record and California crash landed back to earth finishing last, giving the Habs the first pick.

9) Toronto Maple Leaf kingpin, Conn Smythe, made many shrewd deals. One of his best was a deal involving a fiery little Irishman from Ottawa named King Clancy. How did Smythe acquire Clancy?

a) On October 18, 1931, Smythe traded Art Smith, Eric Pettinger and $35,000 to Ottawa for Clancy. The deal spelled the end for the Senators, who needed the money in a big way, but, in reality, could not afford to lose that kind of on-ice talent. Within four years, Ottawa had folded. Meanwhile, Clancy went on to help the Leafs win the Cup in 1932 and make the finals three out of the next five years.

10) The New York Islanders were defending Stanley Cup champs in 1983 when they selected Pat Lafontaine third over all. How did they acquire that pick?

a) Bill Torrey, Islander GM at the time, made the deal two years before, in October of 1981. He traded Bob Lorimer and Dave Cameron to the Colorado Rockies for their first pick in 1983. By that time, the franchise had transferred and had become the Devils.

11) The Cam Neely deal between Boston and Vancouver was another huge swipe, this time on the Bruins' part. What are the details there?

a) In defence of Canuck GM Jack Gordon, Neely had played three years in Vancouver with one twenty goal season to his credit. He had done little to justify his first round selection. The deal was conducted on June 6,

1986; interestingly Neely's 21st birthday. It included Vancouver's first round pick in 1987, which turned out to be Glen Wesley, and, in return, the Canucks picked up Barry Pederson who was coming off a 76 point season, but was a former two-time 100 point man. He never regained that 100 point form and, early in his fourth year with the Canucks, he was sent to Pittsburgh in a six player deal. Neely, by the way, wore sweater number 21 in Vancouver.

12) Explain how you'd be correct if you said the Montreal Canadiens received Brian Bellows for John Kordic.

a) On November 7, 1988, Montreal traded John Kordic and a sixth round pick to Toronto for Russ Courtnall. After four seasons in Montreal, the Habs unloaded the speedy winger to Minnesota for Brian Bellows in August of '92. Hence the reality of Kordic for Bellows.

13) Two future Hall of Fame goaltenders were traded for each other in a seven player package on June 4, 1963. Name everyone involved.

a) In one of the last transactions Frank Selke Sr conducted for the Canadiens, he sent the temperamental Jacques Plante to the Rangers along with Don Marshall and Phil Goyette for Lorne "Gump" Worsley, Dave Balon, Leon Rochefort and Len Ronson. Marshall and Plante had both been members of the "five Cups in a row" of the late 1950s; Goyette was there for four of them. Worsley enjoyed his first team success after years of struggling with the Rangers.

14) What former first-round selection of the New York Islanders was traded in the Butch Goring deal of 1980?

a) Billy Harris, actually the first Islander ever selected, and Dave Lewis were packaged off to LA for Goring at the trading deadline, March 10, 1980. Goring became a catalyst for the young and improving Islanders, winning the Conn Smythe Trophy in 1981 and playing on all four Stanley Cup winning teams.

15) In the same vein, the Penguins acquired three players from the Hartford Whalers just prior to their run to their first Cup in 1991. Who were they?

a) Same scenario for the Penguins as GM Craig Patrick made a shrewd deal sending John Cullen, Jeff Parker and Zarley Zalapski to Hartford for Ron Francis, Ulf Samuelsson and Grant Jennings. The deal paid dividends for Pittsburgh as all three played roles in the two Cup victories, albeit Jennings in a limited capacity.

16) There have been four cases in the NHL since expansion, where a coach has signed with another team and the old team has received some form of compensation. Red Kelly, when he retired as a player in 1967 and became the first coach of Los Angeles; Fred Shero, when he left Philadelphia for the Rangers; Jacques Demers, when he went from Quebec to St. Louis; and Michel Bergeron, when he went from Quebec to the Rangers. Name the players that were compensation.

a) i) Red Kelly to LA-Ken Block to Toronto
ii) Fred Shero to NY Rangers- a first round pick to Philadelphia which was Ken Linesmen.
iii) Jacques Demers to St. Louis - Gord Donnelly and Claude Julian to Quebec.
iv) Michel Bergeron to NY Rangers - a first round pick which was Daniel Dore and $100,000 to Quebec.

17) The Montreal Canadiens stole one from the Toronto Maple Leafs when they traded their ninth pick from the 1971 draft to Toronto for their second pick in 1975, Doug Jarvis. Who was that player and how many games did he play?

a) Greg Hubick, who played 72 games with the Leafs and five more with Vancouver. Jarvis of course has the NHL record of 964 consecutive games played.

18) What would a chapter on trades be without a question on Dave McIlwain. Name the four teams he played for in one season?

a) Winnipeg, Buffalo, NY Islanders and Toronto, all in the 1991-92 season and all in different Divisions. The Ottawa Senators are his sixth NHL team. He's been traded four times in deals that total over twenty players.

19) Who is the only other NHL player to play for four teams in one season?

a) Dennis O'Brien in 1978, with Minnesota, Colorado, Cleveland and Boston. He was claimed on waivers in every transaction except the one from Colorado to Cleveland, where he was traded for Mike Christie.

20) What NHL player has been traded the most?

a) Without question, Brent Ashton has the record of being involved in eight trades in his career. Ashton's first team was the Vancouver Canucks in 1980.

21) What was the last transaction involving Guy Lafleur?

a) This will catch most people. Minnesota claimed him in the expansion draft May 30, 1991, and so Quebec traded to get him back by sending Alan Haworth to the Stars the next day.

22) Let's break down what must be the most significant trade in sports history, the Wayne Gretzky deal, and see where it takes us. Although Edmonton won another Cup two years after the Gretzky trade, most hockey fans feel that the Oilers have never recouped their losses from the deal. On the accompanying chart, you can see the original deal and all the subsequent trades that have happened. This is called the anatomy of a trade.

The chart might be a little complicated, but what I'm attempting to show is who is left on Edmonton at the start of the 1993/94 season from the original deal involving Gretzky. If your are able to follow it, you'll see that left on the Oilers are the following players, eleven in all:

Igor Kravchuk, Dean McAmmond, Scott Pearson, Craig Fisher, Scott Thornton, Luke Richardson, Shane Corson, Vladimir Vujtek, Todd Elik, Brad Zavisha and the first round pick from 1993, Nick Stajduhar. Using Carson, Gelinas and the draft picks as five separate subsections, follow the chart from left to right checking out each deal that Sather made. There are twelve trades in all and another five transactions. (chart pg18)

23) The Eric Lindros 1992 deal is incredible for sheer enormity for one person. One man for six players, two draft choices and fifteen million American dollars. In effect, it's a nine player deal. Remember it?

a) Peter Forsberg, Steve Duchesne, Kerry Huffman, Mike Ricci, Ron Hextall, Chris Simon, first pick in 1993 (Jocelyn Thibault), and the first pick in the 1994 draft. Quebec lost Huffman for nothing, but the Steve Duchesne with St Louis deal has netted them an extra player already. Hextall and a draft pick were sent to the NY Islanders for Mark Fitzpatrick and a pick.

24) The biggest trade in NHL history was made January 2, 1992; a ten player exchange between Calgary and Toronto. Who is the last player left from the deal on Calgary?

a) Michel Petit is all that remains on Calgary as of this writing. Jeff Reese was sent to Hartford, Gary Leeman to Montreal, Craig Berube went to Washington and Alexander Godynyuk was claimed by Florida. Doug Gilmour, Kent Manderville and Jamie Macoun are still with the Leafs, Rick Wamsley has retired and Ric Nattress was signed as a free agent with Philadelphia.

25) The previous trade is the biggest in terms of actual starters being moved. However, there was one in 1981 that, with the draft choices, totalled eleven men. Which one was it?

a) On July 3, 1981, the Hartford Whalers sent Ray Allison, Fred Arthur, a first, second and third round pick in the 1982 draft to Philadelphia for Rick MacLeish, Blake Wesley, Don Gillen and the Flyers' first, second

Wayne Gretzky
MartyMcSorley *TO LOS ANGELES*
Mike Kruselnyski

Jimmy Carson
Martan Gelinas
1st round picks (1989) (1991) (1993)

1) Jimmy Carson
Keven McClelland *TO DETROIT*
5th round pick

Petr Klima ———— To Tampa Bay Futures
Joe Murphy ———— To Chicago for Igor Kravchuk
Dean McAmmond

Adam Graves ——— Signed as Free Agent by N.Y. Rangers
Edmonton receives Troy Mallette - Traded to New Jersey for David Maley ——— David Maley
Jeff Sharples ——— Traded to New Jersey for Reijo Ruotsalainen (since retired)   claimed on waivers by San Jose

2) Martin Gelinas   *TO QUEBEC*

Scott Pearson

3) 1st round pick (1989) *TO NEW JERSEY* Cory Foster – Foster
Dave Brown *TO PHILADELPHIA*
Jarri Kurri

Craig Fisher
Scott Mellanby ——— Claimed by Florida
Craig Berube ——— Berube

Vince Damphouse *TO MONTREAL*   Shane Corson
Glenn Anderson *TO TORONTO* Peter Ing ——(bought out of contract) Brent Gilchrest *TO MINNESOTA*   Todd Elik
Grant Fuhr   Scott Thornton   Vladmir Vujtek
   Luke Richardson

4) 1st round pick (1991)
Martin Rucinsky *TO QUEBEC*

Ron Tugnutt ——— claimed by Anaheim
Brad Zavisha

5) 1st round pick (1993)
Nick Stajduhar

and third round pick in the 1982 draft as well. Two of the draft picks turned out to be Ron Sutter, a first-rounder with the Flyers, and Kevin Dineen, a third-rounder with Hartford.

26) What former General Manager who, as a player, was involved in one of the most embarrassing trades in hockey history?

a) Jake Milford, former GM of the LA Kings from 1974-77, was one of the many players who found out about the legendary Eddie Shore's idiosyncrasies. Shore was the owner and manager of the Springfield Indians when he traded Milford to the Buffalo Bisons for two nets and then complained because of the condition of the nets.

27) The New York Rangers attempted to swing a deal for Eddie Shore in 1928. Who did they try to trade and what was the response from Boston Bruin General Manager Art Ross?

a) Myles J. Lane was one of the few Americans in the NHL in the late 1920s. Lester Patrick attempted to deal him to the Bruins for superstar Eddie Shore. Ross' reply was, "you're so many Myles from Shore you need a life preserver."

Eventually Lane was sold to the Bruins in the 1928-29 season where he played on their Cup winner in 1929. Forty years later, Lane began a new career when he was named as a New York State Supreme Court Judge on January 1, 1969.

28) Who was the first Hart Trophy winner to be traded after winning the trophy?

a) Herb Gardiner, a defenceman with the Montreal Canadiens, won the Hart Trophy in 1927. At the start of the 1928-29 season, he was traded to Chicago for Art Lesieur. He became the playing coach for Chicago that season.

29) Who were the players involved in the Dale Hunter deal, which saw him go from Quebec to Washington?

a) On June 13, 1987, the Nordiques dealt their heart and soul, Dale Hunter, along with goaltender Clint Malarchuck to the Capitals for Gaetan Duchesne, Alan Haworth and a first-round pick, which turned out to be Joe Sakic.

SO YOU THINK YOU'RE RIGHT

If I had a dollar for the number of times I've corrected people on the following questions, I'd be a millionaire. See if you thought you were right about some of these, only to find out it ain't necessarily so.

1) On February 11, 1971, Jean Béliveau scored his 500th career goal against Minnesota. Who was the goaltender?

a) Béliveau's historic marker was scored against Gilles Gilbert, not Caesar Maniago like most people believe. He was assisted by Frank Mahovlich and Phil Roberto and it was his third goal of the night in a 6-2 win.

2) Bobby Baun scored a Stanley Cup winning goal for Toronto on a broken leg sometime in the 1960s.

a) Well it was the 1960s – April 23, 1964, to be exact – but other than that, the facts are a little mixed up. First of all, it was not a Stanley Cup winning goal but a goal that won Game Six in overtime sending the series to Game Seven, which the Leafs won 4-0. Secondly, Baun had a fractured ankle not a broken leg. He had it frozen prior to his game winning goal and did not have it x-rayed until after the series. This is not meant to diminish Baun's accomplishments, which were amazing all the same, it's just a clarification.

3) Stan Mikita led the league in penalty minutes one season and won the Lady Byng trophy the next year.

a) Very close, however, it's not true. In 1964, Mikita and Terry Harper were tied at 149 pim's each. A mere minor penalty away from the leader, Vic Hadfield, who had 151. The following year, he had 154 minutes which placed him sixth on the overall list. Carl Brewer led with 177. Mikita's decline began the following year, 1966, when he had a mere 58. And then, in the next two seasons, when he did actually win the Lady Byng Trophy, he had 12 and 14 minutes respectively.

4) Jacques Plante was the first goaltender to wear a mask.

   a) Not even close on this one. Plante first wore his mask on November 1, 1959, in a game against the Rangers. Clint Benedict of the Montreal Maroons was the first when he wore a leather mask to protect his nose, which had been broken. On February 27, 1930, in a game against the Detroit Falcons, Benedict wore the mask only to lose it in a scramble and once again have his nose broken. That was it for him. He retired and never played another game. James "Flat" Walsh finished the season for the Maroons.

5) Michel Bergeron is the youngest coach in the history of the NHL.

   a) Guess what gang? There are two Michel Bergerons. One was a player born November 11, 1954, the other was a coach born June 12, 1946. Therefore, that makes coach Bergeron 34 when he began his duties with the Quebec Nordiques. Gary Green remains the youngest coach ever at 26 years of age with the Washington Capitals when he was appointed November 14th.1979.

6) Who tripped Bobby Orr when he scored his historic goal, May 10, 1970, against the St Louis Blues?

   a) Most people will tell you that it was Barclay Plager however, the real answer is Noel Picard.

7) Gordie Howe and his brother Vic are the highest scoring brother combination.

   a) Obviously this is no longer the case with Brent Gretzky picking up a couple of points in the 1993-94 season. Still, the Howes have not had the record since 1971. Early in the 71-72 season, after Henri Richard had picked up two points, the Richards were the highest scoring brothers for total regular season points. The Howes were actually passed by the Mahovlichs as well. For argument's sake, let's leave it at families. Here are the top three:

		REGULAR SEASON	INCLUDING PLAYOFFS
Sutters	(6)	2,689	2,956
Howes	(4)	2,600	2,823
Hulls	(3)	2,427	2,705

These totals include points accumulated to the end of the 1993 season. As mentioned, Brent Gretzky's points in the 93-94 season now make him and Wayne eligible however, even with Wayne's totals of 2,328 in the regular season (2,676 including playoffs) , they would need a few years to catch the Sutters. The Gretzky brothers are the highest two brother combination to this point in the NHL.

8) What Stanley Cup final took the longest time to play before the winning goal was scored?

a) Pete Babando's overtime winner in 1950 with Detroit, the first year a final went seven games and into overtime, is always referred to as the longest. However, this is not true. Babando's was scored at 8:31 of the second overtime period, while Harold "Mush" March's winner in 1934 was scored at the 10:05 mark of the second overtime period in Game Four, helping the Hawks beat Detroit three games to one.

9) Lanny McDonald was the first person to score 200 goals or more with two different teams.

a) Wrong again. Phil Esposito scored 459 goals with the Bruins and 219 with the NY Rangers. He retired before Lanny was even traded to Calgary, which was the second team he scored 200 with.

10) The Chicago Black Hawks were the only team to win the Stanley Cup with a sub .500 record.

a) Not true. The Toronto Maple Leafs of 1949 equalled that record by winning the Cup after a regular season of 22-25-13. Chicago in 1938 were 14-25-9.

11) Who was the last playing coach in the NHL?

a) Most people who would hazard a guess think it was Doug Harvey with the NY Rangers in 1962. It was actually Charlie Burns with the Minnesota North Stars in 1970. In the dual capacity, Burns had a record of 10-22-12. As a player, that season he was in fifty games and had 3-13-16 totals.

12) Who was the first brother combination to have one as a forward, score on one who was a goaltender?

a) The obvious answer here is the Espositos. Phil on Tony. Guess again. Actually this scenario of one brother shooting on another happened as far back as 1929 when the Thompson brothers faced each other in league play. Paul with the Rangers and Cecil, better known as Tiny, with the Bruins. The Espositos were actually the third such combination. The second one was the Smiths, in 1967. Brian with LA and his brother Gary, the goaltender, who was at that time with the Oakland Seals. Although Brian was only in the NHL briefly, he and Gary are the answer.

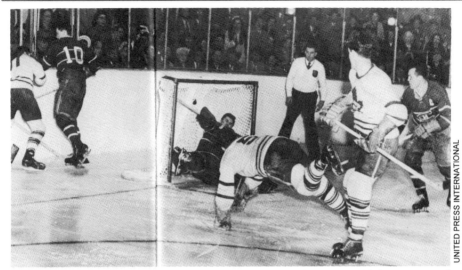

The winning puck flies over the shoulder of Montreal goaltender Gerry McNeil in overtime of the final game. The man who walloped it, Toronto's Bill Barilko (No. 5), watches it even as he topples. Battling on the left are Toronto's Howie Meeker (in white) and Montreal's Tom Johnson, later coach of the Bruins. Looking over Barilko's shoulder is teammate Cal Gardner, while Emile ("Butch") Bouchard, the Montreal captain, observes the worst as it is happening.

13) Bill Barilko scored the Cup winning goal for Toronto in 1951 in overtime and died later that summer in a plane crash. When was the wreckage discovered?

   a) This might disappoint some "Tragically Hip" fans who know that they sing about the crash being found in 1962. It was, however, found on June 7, 1963.

14) The man who scored the first penalty shot goal in the NHL, Ralph (Scotty) Bowman, and the former coach of the Canadiens, Scotty Bowman, are the same person.

   a) This one has been cleared up pretty good, but for a number of years, it was amazing how many people thought they were one and the same man. Ralph Bowman gained hockey immortality on November 13, 1934, while playing for the St Louis Eagles. He scored on a penalty shot against Alex Connell of the Montreal Maroons. Scotty Bowman, the coach, was a little more than a year old when it happened.

Richard, Jean Beliveau and Boom Boom Geoffrion celebrate on way to the Rocket's fifth of eight Stanley Cups in 1957.

15) "Rocket" Richard's best years were during the Second World War, that is before 1945.

a) This statement, uttered by more than just a few people over the years, is completely unfounded and appears to be mostly jeolousy at his and the team's success. True, Richard's best individual season, goal-wise, was 1945 when he had the fifty goal season. However, ten years later, he led the league in goals again with 38, despite being suspended for the last three games of the regular season. All of his league leading, six overtime goals were scored after 1945 and seven of the eight Cup winners he was on were post 1945.

16) What goaltender stopped Wayne Gretzky's point scoring streak at 51 games in 1984?

a) It was the LA Kings; most people get that. However, some think Mario Lessard or Gary Laskowski was the stopper. It was Markus Mattsson on January 28, 1984. In 51 games, Gretzky had 153pts (61G, 92A) .

17) Who has worn number 35 for the Montreal Canadiens in their history?

a) People who are aware that Tony Esposito played for the Canadiens in 1969 assume that he wore number 35. He actually wore number 29. He and Ernie Walkley were the players to wear 29 before Dryden arrived. Also, Danny Geoffrion, son of Bernie, who played briefly in the early 1980's, is thought by many to have worn 35. Not so; he wore number 20. The two 35s, to date, have been Mike McPhee and Greg Moffett.

18) Boston goaltender Dave Reece gained lifetime notoriety when he allowed Darryl Sittler's six goals and ten points. Was that the only game he played in the NHL?

a) Definitely not. It was his last, but he did play thirteen other games and even recorded two shutouts. The season was 1975-76.

19) In the same vein, the goaltender of record the night Bill Mosienko scored his three goals in 21 seconds was Lorne Anderson. Was that his only game in the NHL?

a) On March 23,1952, Lorne Anderson played his last of three NHL games. His record was one win and two losses. However, one of the losses came on that date when Mosienko "caught lightning in a bottle" and scored his record hat trick. Of note that night, he also hit the post on his next rush down the ice and went around the same defenceman, Hy Buller, for all three goals.

20) How many Stanley Cup rings does Reggie Leach have?

a) The obvious answer is two because of the Flyers' consecutive Cup victories. Not so. Leach joined the Flyers on May 24, 1974, in a trade from the California Seals. The Flyers gave up Larry Wright, Al MacAdam and a first-round pick. The deal was done five days after Philadelphia had won their first Cup.

THE BEST OF THE BEST

This is the only chapter in the book where I'll deviate, to a certain extent, from total statistics and trivia. The best of the best in a list of ten players who, in my opinion, have dominated the NHL from its early days in the 1917-18 season, to the present day. Although there will be some statistics, these players have done much more than put impressive numbers on the board. They played the game of hockey with more heart and emotion than seemed humanly possible. Some omissions will spark controversy. However, these are my choices.

JOE MALONE

HOCKEY HALL OF FAME

To most people that peruse the NHL guide, Malone is the name that appears at the top of the list of the year-by-year scoring leaders. The Quebec City native was born February 28, 1890, and had an incredible touch around the net. In 125 NHL games, he scored 146 goals. His numbers are even more impressive when you encompass his pre-NHL days as well: 338 goals in 271 games. On four occasions, he was the scoring leader, including twice in the NHL. He played on three Stanley Cup teams: the Quebec Bulldogs in 1912 and 1913 and the Montreal Canadiens in 1924. Always a clean and sportsmanlike player, he stood out in an era that was dominated by rough play. He didn't possess any one skill that made him better than the rest, he just appeared out of nowhere at the right time and scored. His play earned him the nickname "phantom". As a measure of his leadership and his role on the Quebec team, he was the captain for seven years. To this day, he still holds the NHL record for most goals in one game; seven scored on January 31, 1920, in a 10-6 victory over the Toronto St Pat's. Unfortunately, the game was played on an outdoor rink in Quebec City and the temperature was about -25° F. Only a handful of spectators witnessed history in the making. Malone was inducted into the Hall of Fame in 1950.

Joe Malone Trivia — Malone led the Hamilton Tigers in scoring in their first two years in the NHL in 1921 and 1922.

HOCKEY HALL OF FAME

HOWIE MORENZ

Born September 21, 1902, in Mitchell, Ontario, Morenz cut a swath through the NHL unlike anbody before him. Using blazing speed as his forte, he was acknowledged by everybody as the single most important presence in the game from the mid-1920s until the mid-1930s. It is commonly known that a promoter named Tex Rickard was first turned onto hockey after watching Morenz play. Shortly after that, Rickard founded the New York Rangers. Morenz was a two-time scoring champion and, on three occasions, was the Hart Trophy winner.

MOLSON'S

The Canadiens' magic duo, Howie Morenz (left) and Aurel Joliat, wrap gloves around each other's shoulders. The fiery, 140-pound Joliat played left wing with Morenz at centre. In 1937, while recuperating in a hospital with a broken leg, Morenz died of a heart attack. He was 35.

His passionate dedication to hockey and winning have been a characteristic of all Canadiens teams down through the years.

After falling out of favour with the Montreal management, Morenz was traded to Chicago in 1934, and then to the Rangers in 1936. At the start of the 1936-37 season, he was back with the Habs and rejuvenated playing with his old teammates. On January 28, 1937, he suffered a badly broken leg. Instead of recuperating, he suffered a nervous breakdown and then he developed heart trouble. He died unexpectedly on March 8, 1937, shocking the hockey world. His funeral was held at the Montreal Forum where thousands gathered silently, standing motionless. The second All-Star Game ever was held in his honour on November 7, 1937, at the Forum. Morenz was inducted into the Hall of Fame in 1945.

Howie Morenz Trivia — The reason Howie Morenz wore number 7 is because his first contract was signed on July 7, 1923. That date was team owner and manager Leo Dandurand's birthday, so he suggested Morenz take 7.

EDDIE SHORE

Born in Fort Qu'Appelle, Saskatchewan, on November 25, 1902. Shore was a legend in Western Canada before he played his first game in the NHL. The "Edmonton Express" set precedents for a level of toughness and tolerance of pain that was unheard of. After gaining GM Art Ross' confidence during his first training camp in 1926, Shore set out to make the NHL his personal feeding ground for hysteria. Ross and Shore concocted some of the first public relations moves in hockey history. During warmup and right up until the start of the game, Ross would delay Shore's arrival on the ice. The fans would be unsure of his condition for the game until he would suddenly arrive with the band playing "Hail to the Chief". Shore would be wearing a matador cloak and followed by a valet who would remove the cloak allowing Shore to play. Needless to say, this ploy would drive fans wild.

Shore's many feuds left him quite battered on occasion. On one particular night, he fought five or six Montreal Maroons. Although he never gave an inch, his doctors chart the next day showed a broken nose, three broken teeth, two black eyes, a gashed cheekbone and a two inch cut over his left eye. He played the next game. In a 14 year career, he was a four-time winner of the Hart Trophy. Had there been a Norris Trophy back then, he probably would have won it ten times. He helped the Bruins to two Stanley Cups and was inducted into the Hall of Fame in 1945.

Eddie Shore Trivia — He scored his final goal as a Bruin, December 5, 1939. Early in 1940, he was traded to the New York Americans for Eddie Wiseman and cash.

HOCKEY HALL OF FAME

Eddie Shore stands forbiddingly before the nets. The combative Edmonton Express was nearly as well known as football's Red Granger and baseball's Babe Ruth. "There are people," said one writer, "who have never seen a hockey game who know who Eddie Shore is".

MAURICE RICHARD

Born August 4, 1921, in Montreal, Quebec, Richard was the catalyst for the birth of a Montreal 'style' of hockey that continued for forty-plus years - firewagon hockey. His passion for sports was fuelled during his early days at home in Bordeaux, a suburb in North Montreal. Excelling in baseball and hockey, Richard even entered a Golden Glove Boxing tournament and did quite well, which opponents on the ice would find out about to their surprise for years to come. After several setbacks due to injury, he exploded on the scene in 1943-44 scoring 32 goals in the regular season and helping the Habs win the Cup with another 12 goals in nine playoff games. Put on a

DAVE BARBOUR, MOLSON'S

"His eyes glowed like a rocket's red glare". A quote from sportswriter Andy O'Brien.

line with Hector "Toe" Blake and Elmer Lach, the trio became known as the "Punch Line" and, two years later, they led the Canadiens to another Stanley Cup.

The zeal and passion with which the superstars before Richard played the game were magnified in the Rocket because he carried the hopes and dreams of an entire people, the French Canadians. He scored on end-to-end rushes, going through entire teams; he knocked out some of the toughest players in the game with one punch; he hit referees on or off the ice; and he led the Montreal Canadiens to unprecedented heights. He was the first man to score fifty goals in a season, the first to score 500 in a career and the Captain of the Canadiens when they set the record of five Stanley Cups in a row.

And, of course, there was the riot. Precipitated by a Richard suspension in 1955, never before or since has the entire hockey world been so drawn to an incident regarding one man. Suspended for a fight where he broke two sticks over an opponent and then punched a linesman, Richard had to appear on TV and radio to calm the people down after they destroyed many businesses in the core of the city of Montreal, causing damages worth millions of dollars. He was the second person to have the minimum waiting period of three years waived for entry into the Hall of Fame when he was inducted in 1961, the year after he retired. Regarded as possibly the purest goal scorer in the game, and the most dominant player from the blue line to the net in hockey history, there will always be only one "Rocket", Maurice Richard.

"Rocket" Richard Trivia — There's not much that people don't know or that hasn't been written about him. However, one fact that isn't heard often is that the "Rocket"scored the second fastest game winning goal in NHL history (regular season - Charlie Conacher, February 6, 1932; 7 seconds, Toronto 6 - Boston 0). On January 1, 1952, he scored the first goal in a 3-0 Montreal victory over Chicago, 12 seconds into the game. Not only that, but it was on a penalty shot. The goalie was Harry Lumley.

GORDIE HOWE

Born March 31, 1928, in Floral, Saskatchewan, Gordie Howe defied all logic by playing a 32 year pro hockey career that spanned five decades. The fourth of nine children, Howe quit school early to work in construction. At the age of 15, he took an overnight train to Winnipeg where he attended his first training camp, that of the New York Rangers. The well-known story had Howe becoming homesick and returning home. However, the next year, after an invitation to the Red Wings camp in Windsor, Ontario, he was offered his first contract by Jack Adams, GM of the Wings. It would be two years before Howe would suit up for the parent club but, by then, he was a strapping, slope-shouldered, six-footer weighing 205 lbs. Like the Dennis Hopper commercial for Buffalo Bill Lineman Bruce Smith, Howe did "bad things man, bad things". It wasn't until his fifth year in the league that he

WITH PERMISSION OF JOHN HALLIGAN

Howe in his prime with the Red Wings.

had more points than penalty minutes in a season. The change might have been prompted by a conversation with Adams who said, "Gordie, we know you can fight but can you play the game?" Play he did. He lead the league in scoring the next four years and then twice more in the next nine. Along the way he came within one goal of the "Rocket's" record of fifty goals when he scored 49 in 1953. He did, however, set a record for points with 95 that stood for six years.

Although his name is on four Stanley Cups he was active on only three, after a serious injury in the 1950 playoffs nearly killed him.

It would turnout that very little could stop Howe. Although Detroit haven't won a Cup since 1955, Howe played out his career there, retiring in 1971, only to come back in the WHA during the 1973-74 season and play with his sons. Absolutely unheard of. Would the 45 year old embarrass himself and the game of hockey? Not likely. Twice in six seasons he topped the 100 point mark; on another occasion he had 99. Howe retired after one more year in the NHL where he played all 80 games, scored 15 goals, turned 52 and became a grandfather.

The man known as "Mr Hockey" has been perhaps the greatest ambassador of the game in history. Although never flashy or dramatic, like his rival "Rocket" Richard or several superstars past or present, Howe was regarded at one time as the greatest athlete in the world. Gretzky and company have eclipsed his scoring records, but his longevity and durability, combined with a high excellence of play, will never be equalled. Howe was inducted into the Hall of Fame in 1972, like the "Rocket", with the waiting period waived.

Gordie Howe Trivia — Howe's last regular season goal was scored when he was a Hartford Whaler on April 6, 1980, at 11:25 of the second period against his old team, the Red Wings. He was assisted by Ray Allison, who was born a month before Gordie turned 21, and Gordie Roberts, who was named after Gordie by his mother who was a huge Red Wing fan. He scored the goal on Rogie Vachon who was one year and one month old when Gordie scored his first goal in the NHL.

BOBBY HULL

Born on January 3, 1939, in Pointe Anne, Ontario, Robert Marvin Hull, nicknamed the "Golden Jet", burst on the NHL scene during the 1957-58 season. If you look closely at the TV footage of "Rocket" Richard's 500th career goal on October 19, 1957, you'll notice a young looking number sixteen skating off the ice into the Chicago bench, after the "Rocket" is being congratulated. It was Hull's fifth career game and who could know that he

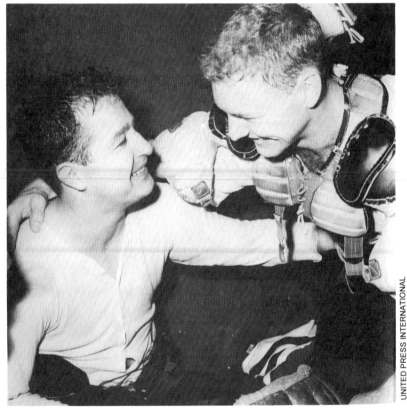

On the eve of the final series against Detroit, Chicago's Glenn Hall (left) and a young Golden Jet, Bobby Hull, congratulate each other after the Black Hawks eliminated Montreal in the semifinal round.

would later be the man to beat the "Rocket's" record of fifty goals in one season and also surpass his career mark of 544 regular season goals.

Hull combined tremendous speed with raw power and strength. After a stellar junior career in St. Catharines, he was expected to pay immediate dividends in Chicago and he did. His first year, he finished runner-up to Frank Mahovlich for the Calder Trophy. His third season, at the age of twenty-one, he won his first scoring championship. The following year, 1961, he won his one and only Stanley Cup and, the year after that, he had his first fifty goal season. With the curved blade added to his repertoire, he now possessed a shot that not only travelled about 100 m.p.h. but had movement. A goaltender's nightmare. During 1965-66, he became the first man to score fifty goals on more than one occasion and then, on March 12, he broke the record which had stood for 21 years when he scored his 51st goal of the season.

His scoring and his shot are legendary but the measure of the man is best described by the instant credibility he gave the fledgling WHA in 1972. It was without question, the most significant development in hockey history. Winnipeg was so enamoured with him they took their name, the Jets, from his nickname "The Golden Jet". He was greeted as a national hero and he repaid them by taking the Jets right to the top of their division. He scored 303 goals in 411 games. Although the NHL looked down upon the upstart organization, which lasted seven seasons, several prominent hockey people got their start there, notably Jacques Demers, Mark Messier and Wayne Gretzky.

History regards Hull as the greatest left winger to play the game. The three time scoring champ and two time league MVP was inducted into the Hall of Fame in 1983. Bobby and his son Brett are the only father-and-son combination to win the Hart Trophy.

Bobby Hull Trivia — When Hull became the first man to score fifty goals in a season for the second time, he scored the big goal (number 50) against Hank Bassen of the Detroit Red Wings. Hank's son, Bob, was a teammate of Brett's for three and a half years in St Louis.

BOBBY ORR

Robert Gordon Orr was born on March 20, 1948, in Parry Sound, Ontario. At the age of 12, he was put on the Bruins' protected list and, from that moment, the hopes and dreams of Boston management and their fans were centred on the arrival of the prodigy. By 14, he was in the tough Ontario major junior league with the Oshawa Generals. After a phenomenal junior career, he arrived at the Bruin training camp a scared stiff 18 year old. The accolades immediately heaped on the young man were overwhelming. The Bruins were coming off a string of seven straight seasons of missing the playoffs. Orr would

HOCKEY HALL OF FAME

lead them to the promised land. Well, so they thought. Although he won the Calder Trophy that season, the Bruins missed the playoffs for an eighth time and actually had a worse record than the years before. No matter, the seeds were sown. The Phil Esposito deal was the final piece to the puzzle and, in the next three seasons, the Bruins were quarterfinalists, semifinalists and finally in 1970, Stanley Cup Champions for the first time in 29 years. THE GOAL was scored by number 4, Bobby Orr, and is regarded by many as the number one playoff goal of all-time. Certainly scoring in overtime

and then flying through the air made it exciting to watch. Throughout the remainder of his all-too-brief career, Orr had many people convinced, and with justification, that he was not only the greatest defenceman of all time, but perhaps the greatest player of all time. His three Hart Trophies for league MVP were surpassed by both Howe and Shore and equalled by Morenz (don't forget this was before number 99). However, for a defenceman to lead the league in scoring, which he did twice, that was unbelievable.

Orr had the best traits of all the greats rolled into one. He controlled a game like Doug Harvey; he could shoot, not like Hull but he could fire it; had great speed and manoeuvrability, like Hull and Morenz; he had the

HOCKEY HALL OF FAME

competitive desire to win at all costs, like Shore and Richard; and he was deceivingly tough, like Howe. Most of Orr's records have been surpassed but the way he dominated the game in the late 1960s and early 1970s will never be forgotten by those who saw him play. He was inducted into the Hall of Fame in 1979, the same season he retired. Again, a first for Robert Gordon Orr.

Bobby Orr Trivia — Although plus-minus statistics were not kept prior to 1968, it's a safe bet that Orr's record in 1971 was not broken. In that year, he set a record for defencemen of 139 points including 102 assists but, more impressively, his plus-minus was +124. It remains a record to this day.

HOCKEY HALL OF FAME

GUY LAFLEUR

Born on September 20, 1951, in Thurso, Quebec, Lafleur was the continuation of French superstars on the Montreal Canadiens after "Rocket" Richard and Jean Béliveau. Like Orr, Lafleur was being watched as early as twelve years old, especially after his performance at the prestigious Quebec City Peewee tournament in 1963. However, unlike the gregarious Bobby Hull or aggressive Bobby Orr, Lafleur channelled his talent into an intense almost brooding attitude. Lafleur lived for the rink and the game and only that. Without the familiarity of his home, family, friends and teammates, his adjustment to junior hockey in Quebec City was difficult. These same

HOCKEY HALL OF FAME

feelings would be evident four years later when he once again had to make the transition from junior in Quebec City, where he was now quite comfortable, to the "show" in Montreal. The pressure was smothering, it was immediate and it was all encompassing. It began with his sweater number. He had worn 4 throughout his entire hockey life and now here he was replacing Béliveau on the roster and being asked if he wanted the famous number 4. Undecided, Lafleur spoke to"Le Gros Bill" and was advised that he could take 4 if he wanted, but it would be better to take a new number and make it his own. It was a saving grace in a season that would test management, fans and

HOCKEY HALL OF FAME

Lafleur himself. The helmeted Lafleur struggled his first three years, although the team wrapped a couple of quarterfinal defeats around a Stanley Cup in 1973. With the beginning of the 1974-75 season, the "Flower" began to bloom. No helmet, a new contract and a wife are cited as some of the reasons for the emergence of Guy Lafleur, superstar. Six straight fifty goal seasons (at that time a record), six straight first All-Star team selections, three scoring titles, two Hart Trophies, a Conn Smythe Trophy and four more Stanley Cups, all in a row. He was the game's most dominant player and he did it with a blazing style; hair flowing behind him as he streaked down the ice firing that patented slap shot from the top of the circle.

HOCKEY HALL OF FAME

The circumstances that led to Lafleur's retirement from the Canadiens in 1984 are well documented. Suffice to say, that the transition of the team from 1979 to 1980 was too much for any organization to bear and the crumbling pieces were left dangling on Lafleur's shoulders. After injuries both on and off the ice, and with the ever present media and fan choke-hold, Guy could take no more and packed it in on November 26, 1984. In hindsight, was it the right thing to do? Under those circumstances and in that situation, no question. Could the man still play the game, absolutely! Hollywood could not have written a better script with Lafleur's comeback. Especially in his first game back at the Forum when he scored twice in a Ranger uniform on February 4, 1989, and finally in a Nordique uniform, on March 30, 1991, where he scored again and the chorus rang down from above, "Guy, Guy, Guy, Guy". He was inducted into the Hall of Fame in 1988, so his comeback made him only the second man in hockey history, besides Gordie Howe, to play after being inducted into the Hall.

Guy Lafleur Trivia—Lafleur never had a five-goal game in the NHL and only had one four goal game. That was January on 26, 1975, in a 7-2 win over the Penguins. One other little stat, his first All-Star game he didn't wear number 10, but 16 instead. Carol Vadnais wore 10 because of seniority.

WAYNE GRETZKY

Born on January 26, 1961, in Brantford, Ontario, this man was destined to change forever the game of hockey. Let's face it, how many kids score 378 goals in one year as a ten year old. He was skating at two and snapping them upstairs to the top shelf when he was three. Well maybe a slight exageration, but not by much. His accomplishments are overwhelming. He has led in scoring, every tournament he has ever played in, from the time he was a child right up to and including every Canada Cup. He owns more than sixty NHL individual records and has dominated both the Art Ross Trophy and the Hart Trophy like no man before him. He has enjoyed team success with

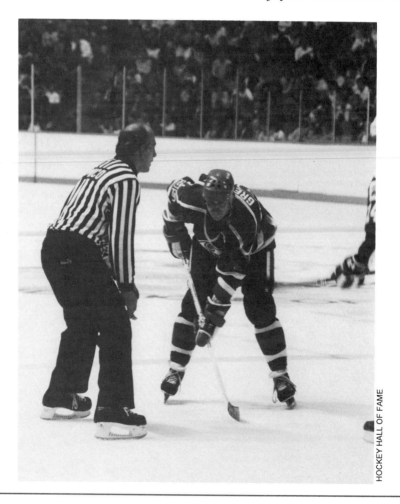

HOCKEY HALL OF FAME

HOCKEY HALL OF FAME

four Stanley Cup rings from his Edmonton days and most recently led the LA Kings to the finals for their first time in 1993 by setting another standard for himself by leading the playoffs in goals, assists and points for the first time in his career. Like Morenz, 65 years before him, he is singularly responsible for League expansion in the South and has opened up roads for the game to go where before were only dead ends.

To pare away everything but the most basic of reasons for this phenomenon, one must look at the man on skates, holding a stick and cradling a puck. Wayne Gretzky plays the game on the ice but watches it unfold from somewhere up above. No amount of practice or hard work can teach a human being to be that aware of his surroundings in their work environment. What the normal player sees unfolding before him, number 99 has seen, digested, calculated and compensated for. To give one example is almost unfair, but his play in the Canada Cup of 1987, where he not only elevated his level but that of Mario Lemieux's in what has been described as the greatest three-game series in hockey history, was one of many significant accomplishments. With Lemieux's day-to-day presence on the ice tenuous at best, Gretzky has maintained his place atop the heap, so to speak, rolling on towards what few individual goals escape him and attempting to achieve that one final moment of shining glory – a Stanley Cup in LA.

Wayne Gretzky Trivia — Do you know this name, 'Brian Gulazzi'. He is the man responsible for Gretzky wearing number 99. He was wearing 9 on the Sault Ste Marie Greyhounds when Wayne arrived and would not give it up. After experimenting with 14 and 19, Gretzky eventually settled in with 99. The rest is history.

HOCKEY HALL OF FAME

MARIO LEMIEUX

Born October 5, 1965, in Montreal, Quebec, Mario Lemieux grew up idolizing Guy Lafleur. Raised in Laval, Mario would eclipse all of his idol's records in the Quebec Major Junior Hockey League and then leave everybody, but one, behind in his assault on the NHL record book. The comparisons with Gretzky were inevitable on the ice. Off it, Lemieux was a distant second in dealing with the public and the media. The turning point everybody alludes to is the 1987 Canada Cup. After several refusals to play for his country, he teamed up with Wayne and Company on maybe the greatest collection of

HOCKEY HALL OF FAME

talent ever assembled on one team. It's said that Gretzky showed him the way to prepare and, in doing so, assisted on nine of the tournament leading eleven goals Lemieux scored. Lemieux exploded for his first seventy-goal season following the Canada Cup and then, the following year, finally led the Penguins into the post season with a Gretzky-like season of 199 points. Although the best was yet to come, team wise, Mario has not played more than sixty-four games in a season since. With 1993's startling news of

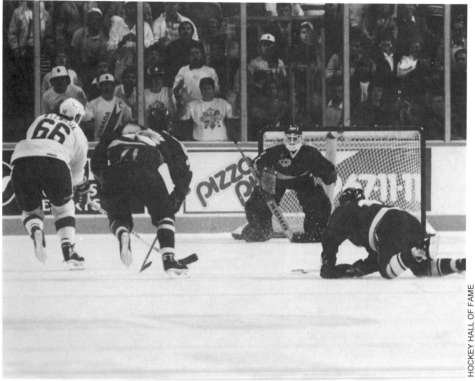

HOCKEY HALL OF FAME

Hodgkins disease and his continued trouble with his back, he may never play a full season again.

The Penguins' championship seasons of 1991 and 1992 allowed Lemieux the opportunity to shine like the superstars before him, but it has left the hockey world hungry for more. He cruises effortlessly with the puck using his size and strength to work himself into the pivotal position for either the perfect pass or a laser shot to his favourite spot – top corner, glove side. His goals were highlight film material and his incredible comeback from treatment for Hodgkins to overtake Pat Lafontaine for the scoring championship in 1993 is the stuff legends are made of. What the future holds for Mario Lemieux and the Penguins is dependent on how much the fans and the media allow him to contribute in a limited role, possibly for the remainder of his career. If it's only a brief glimpse throughout the season then a herculean effort in the playoffs, so be it. He is the Magnificent One and his place in history is secure.

Mario Lemieux Trivia — Mario Lemieux and Kevin Stevens became the first teammates to score fifty goals in a season in the same game; on March 21, 1993, in a 6-4 victory over Edmonton, they scored on goaltender Ron Tugnutt. Not only that, but the game was played at a neutral location in Cleveland.

HOCKEY HALL OF FAME

STANLEY CUP ODDITIES

The ultimate goal of every player and every team is Lord Stanley's mug. It was originally purchased for $48.67 and first awarded in 1893 to the Montreal Amateur Athletic Association. The man himself, Lord Stanley, at the time Governor General of Canada, never saw a hockey game. Little did he know what a gift he had given to the future of our great country. Some of the best questions are playoff questions. Try these ones on for size.

1) When was the only time three brothers played on a Stanley Cup winning team?

a) In 1903, the Ottawa "Silver Seven" won the Stanley Cup in a playoff with the Montreal Victorias. They then defended it in a two-game series against Rat Portage. Three Gilmour brothers, Dave, S.C. (Suddy) and Bill, were key players in the "Silver Seven" triumph. It was the only time all three played together.

2) Frank McGee's legendary game of 1905, with the same Ottawa Silver Seven, saw him score a record 14 goals in one game. It was the second of a two game series. How many did he score in the first game and what was the score?

a) The two-game series was played against the Dawson City Nuggets, also known as the Klondikers. Game One was a 9-2 Ottawa win with McGee getting one goal. Game Two was 23-2. The goaltender was a young man named Albert Forrest, 17 years old. He was the youngest goalie in Stanley Cup history. McGee, by the way, had sight in only one eye.

3) When was the first time that two goaltenders shared a shutout in the playoffs?

a) March 22, 1955, the Montreal Canadiens, coached by Dick Irvin Sr, beat Boston 2-0. He used both Charlie Hodge and Jacques Plante for the victory.

4) Some say Terry Sawchuck's play in the 1952 playoffs might have been one of the greatest goaltending displays of all time. What was his record and his average?

a) Sawchuck was a perfect 8-0, allowing only five goals for 0.63 average. He also had four shutouts, including back-to-back shutouts in the final against Montreal.

Tony Leswick, Terry Sawchuck and Ted Lindsay celebrate Game One, 1952 Finals.

5) Why was Toronto's triumph in 1932 referred to as the "Tennis Series"?

a) The Leafs beat the NY Rangers in the finals three straight by scores of 6-4, 6-2, 6-4.

6) Many have heard the story of King Clancy playing every position in a Stanley Cup game. Is it true, and if so, when was it?

a) Well obviously by the question it's true and it is a great story. The Ottawa Senators beat a team called the Edmonton Eskimos two straight in a best of three, late March of 1923. Game One was won by a 2-1 score. Game Two 1-0. It was in Game Two, on March 31, that Clancy gained his fame. In those days, the players played the whole game, or close to it. A sub was in briefly, if at all. Clancy replaced Eddie Gerard and George "Buck" Boucher in the first period. In the second, he spared for Frank Nighbor and Cy Denneny. Finally, in the third, he spelled Harry "Punch" Broadbent and in the dying minutes, after goaltender Clint Benedict drew a minor for slashing, Clancy replaced him. In those days, goaltenders also served their penalties.

7) 1919 is the only year without a Stanley Cup winner. The story is well known about the Spanish Influenza epidemic forcing the cancellation of the series. However, NHL president Frank Calder wanted to award the Stanley Cup to Seattle. Why?

a) Because it would be a precedent call to have no champion, Calder was determined to have a winner. He felt that, even though the teams were tied after five games with two wins and a tie each, Seattle should get the Cup because they had outscored Montreal 19 goals to 10. Seattle Manager Frank Patrick refused to accept the trophy under those conditions, so that's why there is no winner for that year.

Richard turns on former teammate Ivan Irwin durning the 1956 semi-finals.

8) When was the first time "Rocket" Richard was suspended in the playoffs?

   a) During the 1947 final between the Canadiens and the Leafs. Richard was suspended for Game Three after an altercation in Game Two where he, "slashed shut the eye of Vic Lynn and cut open Bill Ezinicki's skull." The quote is from the Trail of the Stanley Cup, Volume Two. The Leafs went on to win the series.

9) Who was the youngest person to score a Stanley Cup winning goal?

   a) In that same 1947 series, Game Six, won by the Leafs 2-1, a young twenty year old by the name of Ted "Teeder" Kennedy scored the winning goal. The second youngest was Mario Tremblay of the Canadiens who was 21 when he scored the deciding goal in Game Six, 1978, against the Boston Bruins. The score was 4-1.

10) Name the four players who were on the last Stanley Cup won by Detroit in 1955 and the last one the Toronto Maple Leafs won in 1967.

a) Terry Sawchuck, Red Kelly, Larry Hillman and Marcel Pronovost.

11) The man who scored the goal in the longest game ever played shares another unique distinction in regards to overtime. What is it?

a) Modère "Mud" Bruneteau, who scored to decide the longest game in 1936, and his brother, Ed, are the only brother combination to score overtime goals in the same playoff year, 1945. "Mud" scored against the Bruins in the semi-final won by his team, the Detroit Red Wings. Ed, playing for the Wings as well, scored against the Leafs in the final which was won by Toronto.

12) What are the other brother combinations to score overtime goals in the playoffs?

a) The Cooks, Bill and Bun (Fred); the Richards, Maurice and Henri; the Sutters, Daryll, Brent and Duane; and the only father – son combination, the Hulls, Bobby and Brett.

13) What player played the longest NHL career without ever playing in the playoffs?

One half of the Bruneteau brothers, Mud, shown, here in 1945.

WITH PERMISSION OF JOHN HALLIGAN

a) Guy Charron played 734 regular season games and never once saw playoff action. Unfortunately, he was with the Montreal Canadiens organization in 1970, which was the last year they missed the playoffs.

14) Who was the only goaltender to captain a Stanley Cup winning team?

a) Chuck Gardiner with the Chicago Black Hawks in 1934.

15) The Chicago Black Hawks were involved in one of the best trivia stories of all time in the playoffs. It was 1938; Chicago was playing Toronto in the finals. Regular Hawk goaltender, Mike Karakas, was injured because of a broken toe and replacement Paul Goodman hadn't arrived, leaving Chicago without a goaltender. With permission from John Devaney, here's the story as told to him by Johnny Gottselig, the Captain of the Hawks at the time.

Chicago owner Major Frederick McLaughlin towers over his star Mush March while congratulating Mush for the goal that won Chicago's first Cup.

"We had a noon meeting before the first game in Toronto that night, and Bill Stewart told us that Mike Karakas couldn't play, his toe was so bad. Our minor league goaltender, Paul Goodman, hadn't arrived. Alfie Moore was a minor league goaltender for Toronto and he lived in Toronto, so Stewart told me to go get him. I knew Alfie. I went to his house and his wife, Agnes, she said he's down at the tavern, you can find him there. I went down to the tavern and a guy told me Alfie just left here, you can find him at another one. I caught him at the second one, and he's sitting there with three or four other hockey players who were through for the season. I walked in and Alfie looked at me and said, 'By God am I glad to see you. I'd love to get a couple of tickets for tonight's game.' And I said, 'Boy, Alfie you got the best seat in the house.' When I told him he was going to play that night, he said, 'Don't give me that bull.' I told him, 'You are playing for sure.' And he said, 'Boy it's about time. That Connie Smythe is going to rue the day he ever sent me down to Pittsburgh. I should have been playing up here instead of Broda, I'll show that Connie Smythe.' Then he said, 'Let's have one more drink on that before we go.' He'd had about ten or a dozen before that. When we brought him back to the hotel, Stewart-he was a non drinker-when he saw him he said, 'get him out of here, he won't play for us tonight.' I said, 'Hell, I'm not going into those nets Bill, and I don't think Mush March will. This guy is going to play or else.' 'Well,' Bill said, 'it's your money fellows, if you want to use this guy go ahead and use him.' We took him out to the rink and put some coffee into him and put him under the shower. By game time he was in pretty good shape. The first shot they threw at him, it went in, the first shot of the game. But after that they couldn't put a puck by him and I guess that night he did show Connie Smythe".

Chicago won the game 3-1 and the series three games to one.

Alfie Moore played a total of twenty-one games in the regular season with the New York Americans and the Detroit Red Wings. He played two other games in the 1939 playoffs with the Americans. Bill Stewart's grandson, Paul Stewart, is currently a referee in the NHL. Johnny Gottselig was the first Russian born player in the NHL and the first Russian born Captain, not Alex Mogilny of the Sabres.

16) The rosters of the teams that have won the Stanley Cup are dotted with players like Alfie Moore, a one-shot wonder, or an extra, who are now a part of hockey history because their name is on the Cup. Here're a couple more for you.

i) Johnny Sherf. Won the Cup in 1937 with Detroit. Played 19 regular season games, no goals; eight playoff games, no goals. Never played in the NHL again.

ii) Stanford Smith. Won the Cup in 1940 with the Rangers. Played one game in the playoffs that year after playing two in the regular season. No goals or points. Played another seven games in 1941.

iii) Phil Samis. Won the Cup with Toronto in 1948; Played five games had one assist.

iv) Chris Hayes. Won the Cup with Boston in 1972. Played one game in the semi-finals against St Louis. It was his only game ever in the NHL.

v) Mike Polich. Won the Cup with Montreal in 1977. Played five games, had no points, played one regular season game in 1978 then signed by Minnesota as a free agent.

vi) Don Awrey. Contrasting the Polich story, he played 72 games in the regular season in 1976 with Montreal. He did not dress for any playoff games and did not get his name on the Stanley Cup.

17) Who was the last playing coach to win the Stanley Cup?

a) Ebbie Goodfellow with the Detroit Red Wings in 1943.

18) In the greatest comeback in the history of the Stanley Cup finals, who scored the Cup winning goal?

a) In 1942, Pete Langelle of the Leafs scored the second goal in a 3-1 final game victory over Detroit. The Leafs had been down three games to none but came back to win the next four. Langelle only scored five goals in a 41 playoff game career. No doubt, that was the biggest.

Toronto's centre Pete Langelle (8) has just fired what proved to be the winning goal in the seventh game of the incredible Stanley Cup comeback scored by the Maple Leafs, April 20, 1942.

UNITED PRESS INTERNATIONAL

19) On the 1980 Stanley Cup winning New York Islanders, there were three Swedish born players. Who were they?

a) Stefan Persson, Anders Kallur and Bobby Nystrom.

20) A player on the 1992 Stanley Cup winning Pittsburgh Penguin team is second to Wayne Gretzky for the most consecutive one hundred point seasons in pro hockey. Who is he?

a) Dave Michayluk who has, to date, nine seasons in a row of one hundred or more points with Kalamazoo, Muskegon and Cleveland.

21) Who scored the Stanley Cup winning goal the last time the New York Rangers won the Cup in 1940?

a) Ron Hextall's grandfather, Bryan Hextall, scored the winner in overtime in Game Six against the Leafs. He was assisted by Phil Watson and Ott Heller.

22) When was the first time that two goaltenders fought in the Stanley Cup finals in the NHL?

a) During Game Two of the finals on April 10, 1948, between the Toronto Maple Leafs and the Detroit Red Wings, Walter " Turk" Broda of the Leafs and Harry Lumley of the Wings squared off after a brawl started on the ice with the main combatants being Gordie Howe and Howie Meeker. No word on the victor, however Lumley enjoyed a significant size advantage. The referee was King Clancy.

A young Henri Richard in his first season with the Canadiens, 1955 – 56

WITH PERMISSION OF JOHN HALLIGAN

23) Game One of the 1952 finals between Montreal and Detroit was an off ice officials' nightmare and had the Habs' Head Coach, Dick Irvin Sr incensed. What happened?

a) The game was played at the Montreal Forum and, mid-way through the third period, Detroit had a 2-0 lead thanks to two goals by Tony Leswick. Tom Johnson scored for the Canadiens cutting the margin to one. When the public address announcer called the last minute of play, Irvin pulled goaltender Gerry MacNeil for an extra attacker. Sid Able set up Ted Lindsay for the empty net goal. The time of the goal was announced as 19:44, sixteen seconds to go in the game. However, after sixteen seconds were played, the clock ran for another minute before the siren went. Officials indicated that there was indeed another minute left and Coach Irvin was livid saying he would not have pulled MacNeil that early had he known. It was to no avail. The goal and the game stood.

24) What was the humorous exchange between defenceman Bill Gadsby of Detroit and goaltender Gump Worsley of Montreal after Game Five of the finals in 1966 won by the Habs 5-1?

a) Gadsby: "Worsley wasn't even tested. His underwear can't even be wet."

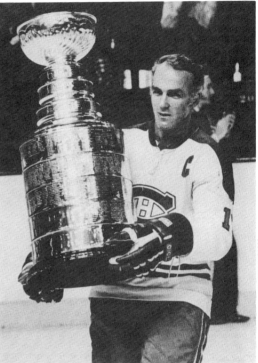

Henri Richard in October of 1973, skates with the Eleventh Cup he won, a record for players

UNITED PRESS INTERNATIONAL

Worsley: "What most people don't know is my underwear is wet before the game even starts."

25) Henri Richard scored the Stanley Cup winner in 1971 in Game Seven against Chicago. It was his second of two in the game which was a 3-2 Montreal victory. Who scored the other goal on a long slap shot after Bobby Hull had just hit the cross bar?

a) Jacques Lemaire, who would go on to score 61 career playoff goals.

26) If there was one playoff goal scored that could rival or surpass Bobby Orr's Stanley Cup overtime winner in 1970, it would be "Rocket" Richard's

WITH PERMISSION OF JOHN HALLIGAN

In a scene that might have been painted by an imaginative artist if it hadn't actually happened and had been photographed: a bloodied Rocket Richard shakes hands with a black-eyed Sugar Jim Henry. Richard's Canadiens had just eliminated Sugar Jim's Bruins in a best-of-seven semifinals.

Game Seven, semi-final goal against the Bruins in 1952. What player knocked the "Rocket" out cold, forcing him out of the game, and what goaltender did he score on when he returned to the game?

a) The reason there even was a Game Seven is thanks to a relatively unknown centre by the name of Paul Masnick. He scored in double overtime in Game Six for the Canadiens to force a Game Seven on April 8. Considering he only scored four playoff goals in his career, it was a big one. Game Seven began with Eddie Mazur of the Habs and Ed Sanford of the Bruins trading goals. The second period was scoreless, but the Canadiens suffered a huge loss when Richard was bowled over by Leo Labine. Richard hit his head on something, either Labine's stick, his skate, the ice or a combination of all three. Regardless, he was badly cut and taken off. With the game still tied at one and in the late stages, Montreal coach, Dick Irvin, noticed the "Rocket" had taken his spot on the bench. He sent him out there and everybody in the rink witnessed one of the many moments that made the "Rocket" a legend. Taking a pass deep in his own end from Butch Bouchard, the "Rocket" headed up ice. He swept around or through four Bruins before he found himself alone in front of goaltender Sugar Jim Henry. He rifled a low shot by him for the game and what would be the series winning goal. Billy Reay added an insurance marker for a final score of 3-1. Boston Bruin coach, Lynn Patrick, was quoted as saying, "even a truck couldn't have stopped Richard on that play." The photo of Bruin goaltender Sugar Jim Henry and the "Rocket" shaking hands is a classic. In a conversation I had with Richard in 1989, he told me that he still does not have any recollection of the goal or the end of the game.

MY TOP QUESTIONS

Following is a list of what I feel are some of the greatest NHL hockey trivia questions of all time.

1) When was the first time that three brothers played on the same line together in the NHL?

   a) During the 1942-43 season, Chicago tried an older Bentley brother, Reg, with his two younger brothers, Max and Doug. The experiment only lasted 11 games and they actually picked up a point together on January 3, 1943, when Reg scored with assists going to his brothers.

2) Prior to the two goalie system, trainers had to sometimes fill in for an injured goaltender. What trainer has the record for the most times filling in?

   a) Ross "Lefty" Wilson, on three occasions for a total of 85 minutes. Once in 1954, for the Detroit Red Wings whom he worked for, once in 1956 for Toronto and again in 1958 for Boston.

3) In 1977, Montreal set a record which may never be broken. They lost only eight regular season games. Only one was at home. Who was it to?

   a) On October 30, 1976, Boston beat them 4-3. It was their only home loss that season.

4) Prior to Bill Mosienko, who had the record for the fastest three goals in regular season play?

   a) Carl Liscombe of the Detroit Red Wings, 64 seconds in 1938.

5) Jimmy Carson set the record for most games played in a regular season with 86 in 1993 in an 84 game schedule. Who has the record for the most games played over and above the regular season number?

a) Although Brad Marsh played 83 games in a season and Doug Crossman 82, Ross Lonsberry has the record with 82 played in a 78 game season in 1972. He played the first fifty games with LA and then was traded to Philadelphia, who had played only 46 at that point. He played the last 32 with them.

6) On November 10, 1963, Gordie Howe broke "Rocket" Richard's record of 544 career goals. Who did he score his 545th against and what were the unusual circumstances?

a) The goal was scored against the Montreal Canadiens. In nets that night was Charlie Hodge. It was a shorthanded goal with Alex Faulkner in the box serving a five minute major. The goal was assisted by Billy MacNeil. MacNeil's birthday is January 26, the same birthday as the man who has been chasing Howe's record for several years, Wayne Gretzky.

7) Who assisted Wayne Gretzky's first goal in the NHL?

a) Brett Callighen and Blair Macdonald at the 18:51 mark of the third period against Glen Hanlon of the Vancouver Canucks. The goal tied the game at four and the date was October 14, 1979.

8) Who were the eight players protected by the four WHA teams when they entered the NHL?

a)
Edmonton	-	Wayne Gretzky, Bengt Gustaffsson
Quebec	-	Paul Baxter, Garry Larivière
Hartford	-	Mark Howe, Jordy Douglas
Winnipeg	-	Scott Campbell, Morris Lukowich

9) In February of 1941, in a game between the Rangers and the Black Hawks, four sets of brothers played. Name them.

a) Lynn and Murray Patrick, Max and Doug Bentley, Neil and Mac Colville, Bill and Bob Carse.

10) Who was runner-up to Bobby Orr for the Calder Trophy in 1967?

a) Ed Van Impe, who was with Chicago at the time. He was drafted by Philadelphia the following year.

11) Name the two players to win the Hart Trophy while playing for last place teams.

a) Tommy Anderson, with the Brooklyn Americans in 1942, and Al Rollins, a goaltender with Chicago in 1954.

12) Name the only two years there were players tied for official All-Star team positions.

a) 1938-Right Wing Gordie Drillon of the Leafs was tied with Cecil Dillon of the Rangers.
1951-The second team centre position was a tie between Sid Able of Detroit and Ted Kennedy of Toronto. The first team spot was held by Milt Schmidt of Boston.

13) Which Original Six team was the first to lose a playoff round to an expansion team?

a) The New York Rangers in 1974 lost a seven game series to the eventual Stanley Cup champions, Philadelphia.

14) Who was Captain of the Montreal Wanderers during their brief stay in the NHL?

a) Art Ross, the man the trophy is named after, was Captain for the short time they were in existence. When their home rink, the Westmount Arena burned down on January 2nd of 1918, the franchise folded.

15) Who assisted on Bobby Hull's record breaking 51st goal of the season on March 12, 1966?

a) Bill Hay and Lou Angotti assisted the famous goal. It was an unusual assist because Angotti, after getting the puck from Hay, passed it to Hull in his own zone and then went to the bench on a line change. Hull took the puck end-to-end and scored on a slapshot from just over the blue line.

16) Denis Savard was on a very unique line in junior hockey. They all shared the same first name and the same birth date. What were his linemates' names and when was their birthday?

a) Denis Cyr and Denis Tremblay were his linemates on the Montreal Canadiens Juniors. The line was known as "Les trois Denis". Their birthday is February 4, 1961. Denis Tremblay never made the NHL. Denis Cyr played 193 games in the NHL with three teams: Calgary, St Louis and two seasons in Chicago.

17) With all the high scoring in the All-Star Games now, it's hard to imagine a shutout. As a matter of fact, there has been only one shutout in the history of All-Star competition? When was it and who recorded it?

a) It was in 1967, as the defending Stanley Cup Champions, the Montreal Canadiens, shutout the All-Star team 3-0. The goose egg was split between Charlie Hodge and Gary Bauman. Interestingly, in a brief NHL career that spanned only 35 games, Bauman never recorded a shutout.

18) What two players are the only ones to score their 50th goal of the season on their birthday?

a) Phil Esposito and Wayne Gretzky. Esposito's birthday is February 20 and, on three occasions, he popped number 50 on that day. Once against his brother Tony in 1972. Gretzky managed the unique feat the sixth time he recorded a fifty goal season on January 26, 1985, the day he turned 24. He scored the goal against Dennis Herron of the Penguins.

19) Who was the last player to lead his team in one season in all categories, goals, assists, points and penalty minutes?

a) Stan Smyl with the Vancouver Canucks in 1980. He had 31 goals, 47 assists, 78 points and 204 pim.

20) What are the two lowest draft choices to become captain of an NHL team?

a) Dave Taylor of the LA Kings was drafted 210th overall in 1975 and was captain of the Kings from 1986-1989. Dan Frawley was drafted 204th overall in 1980 by Chicago and was captain of Pittsburgh during the 1987-88 season.

21) The man who preceded Max Bentley on the Pony Line was also the first winner of the Lady Byng Trophy with two different teams. Who was it?

a) Clint Smith. He won the trophy in 1939 with the Rangers and in 1944 with the Black Hawks. The other two members of the Pony Line were Doug Bentley and Bill Mosienko.

22) The same team drafted the first Russian and the first player from Czechoslovakia. Who were the players drafted and in what years?

a) The team that did the picking was Philadelphia. They drafted Viktor Khatulev in 1975, 160th overall, as the first Russian. Three years later, they took Anton Stastny, 198th overall. However, this created a very special situation as you'll see in my next question.

23) Who was the first player to be drafted twice?

a) This question could have gone in my chapter, "So you think you're right". A lot of people are aware of Joe Reekie being selected by Hartford in 1983 and Buffalo in 1985. A few others know about Rick Corriveau drafted by St Louis in 1989 and Washington in 1991. Both these players were juniors who re-entered the draft. But almost nobody remembers the Anton Stastny situation in 1978. His selection by Philadelphia that year was ruled illegal because of his age. He would have been under 20 had he played that season. If you recall, there was quite a problem between the NHL and the WHA regarding underaged players. Anyway, he went back in the draft the next year, 1979, and was selected by Quebec. He was the first man to be drafted twice.

24) The 1978 Toronto Maple Leafs had one player on their roster whose father played in the NHL, but they used different last names. Who was it and what was the story behind the name change?

a) A young, twenty year old defenceman by the name of Trevor Johansen started his brief NHL career with the Leafs in the 1977-78 season. His father played one game in the NHL for the Leafs as well, during the 1949-50 season. Not wanting to attract any attention because of his Swedish surname, the senior Johansen took the name Johnson. When Trevor came along, Swedes were already making an impact in the league so he had no problem with his real name. Of note, Trevor was involved in a trade along with Don Ashby, which sent them to Colorado for Paul Gardener. Gardener's father was a teammate of Bill Johnson (Johansen) and was a star in the league with the Leafs for several years. His name was Cal Gardner.

25) Who were the three NHL players expelled for life?

a) Billy "The Kid" Taylor and Don Gallinger were expelled in 1948 for conduct prejudicial to and against the welfare of hockey. Essentially, they were gambling on their games and several others. Taylor was with the Rangers at the time, Gallinger with the Bruins. One other player, Billy

Couture of the Boston Bruins, was expelled for life on April 13th, 1927, after attacking referee Jerry Laflamme at the conclusion of their game with the Ottawa Senators. The Senators won the Cup with their victory in that game and at the end there was a huge brawl. While several others fought, Couture made a beeline for Laflamme in full view of League President Frank Calder. Bad idea.

26) In the Hockey Hall of Fame there is only one inductee each in the player category under the letters I, Q, U and V. Who are the players?

a) Dick Irvin Sr under "I", Bill Quackenbush under "Q", Norm Ullman under the "U" and George Vézina under the "V".

27) Bobby Hull broke "Rocket" Richard's record for goals in a season on March 12, 1966. When was Hull's record broken?

a) The same date, March 12, only five years later in 1971. The player was Phil Esposito who was not only a previous teammate of Hull's, but a linemate. Esposito and Hull played on a line in Chicago called the HEM line: Hull, Espo and Chico Maki. Esposito's record stood for nearly eleven years until February 24, 1982, when Gretzky shattered it on way to his 92 goal season. Chico Maki's real name is Ron Maki.

28) During a bad blizzard in New Jersey on the night of January 15, 1983, linesman Ron Foyt had to use two players as officials until referee Ron Fournier and linesman Dan Marouelli showed up. Who did he use?

a) Foyt took one from each team, Garry Howatt from the Devils and Mickey Volcan from the Hartford Whalers.

29) Who was the first American born player to score five goals in a game in the NHL?

a) Mark Pavelich of the Rangers on February 23, 1983, in an 11-3 win over the Hartford Whalers. The goaltender was Greg Millen.

30) What player scored an overtime winner into an empty net during a regular season game?

a) On April 12, 1993, Mike Ridley of the Washington Capitals scored in an empty net at the 4:12 mark against the Canadiens. Montreal had pulled their goalie because they needed the win to try and catch Boston for first place in the division.

31) What player produced the biggest increase in points from one season to the next in the history of the NHL?

a) Bernie Nicholls of the LA Kings, from 1988 to 1989. He went from 78 points to 150 for an increase of 67. Guy Lafleur sits in the number two position, from 1974 to 1975, going from 62 points to 125 for an increase of 63 points.

32) Teemu Selanne smashed Mike Bossy's rookie record of 53 goals ending up with 76. When he scored goal number 54 who was it against and who assisted?

a) Stephane Fiset of the Nordiques was the goaltender and the assists went to Phil Housley and Tie Domi. The date was March 2, 1993, and the Jets lost the game 7-4. By the way, Selanne got a hat trick in the game.

WITH PERMISSION OF JOHN HALLIGAN

Georges Vézina: The first of the great goaltenders he stood in goal for the 1916 Canadiens – the first Flying Frenchmen to win the Cup.

33) When George Vézina collapsed, never to play again, on November 28, 1925, who replaced him in the Montreal nets?

a) Alphonse Lacroix in the interim and then Herb Rheaume finished the season.

34) How much was the salary cap in the NHL in 1925?

a) $35,000 per team except the two new expansion teams, the Pittsburgh Pirates and the New York Americans. They were allowed to exceed the limit by $10,000 all the way to $45,000.

35) On February 7, 1976, Toronto beat Boston 11-4. Darryl Sittler had six goals and four assists. Who scored the Leaf goal that Darryl didn't get a point on?

a) George Ferguson.

36) Who was the last player to score fifty goals or more in a season and not wear a helmet?

a) Al Secord of the Chicago Black Hawks in 1983. He scored it against Mike Palmateer of the Toronto Maple Leafs.

37) What was the last year there were no coaching changes in the NHL?

a) 1967, the year before expansion. The teams and their coaches were:

Montreal	-	Toe Blake
Toronto	-	Punch Imlach
Boston	-	Harry Sinden
Detroit	-	Sid Able
Chicago	-	Billy Reay
NY Rangers	-	Emile Francis

38) What three players played on Stanley Cup winners before they were Calder Trophy winners?

a) Ken Dryden /: Cup winner in 1971, Calder Trophy in 1972.

Tony Esposito /: Cup winner in 1969, Calder Trophy in 1970.

Danny Grant /: Cup winner in 1968, Calder Trophy in 1969

All three were Cup winners with Montreal. Dryden played six regular season games in 1971, winning them all before his twenty playoff games that year. Esposito played 13 games with the Habs in 1969 and had two shutouts. Grant played one game in 1967 and 22 in 1968 before participating in the 1968 playoffs with Montreal.

39) What goaltender had the shortest career in the NHL?

a) Robbie Irons of the St Louis Blues played three minutes in a game during the 1968-69 season. He was basically a third stringer that Scotty Bowman had no choice but to employ one night after Glenn Hall went down with an injury. Jacques Plante was rushed to the rink and, after many stalling techniques used by Bowman and the Blues, he was able to dress and get in the game with Irons only playing the three minutes. He never played another second in the league.

40) Two former fifty goal scorers also led the league in penalty minutes at one time. Who are they?

a) "Rocket" Richard scored fifty goals in 1945 and led the league in penalty minutes in 1953 with 112 minutes. Vic Hadfield led the league in penalty minutes in 1964 with 151 minutes and scored fifty goals in 1972.

41) Who is the only former scoring leader in the history of the NHL to take a turn in the nets for an injured goaltender?

a) Charlie Conacher, who led the league in scoring with the Toronto Maple Leafs in 1934 and 1935, played goaltender on three occasions in his illustrious career. Twice with the Leafs, in 1933 and 1935, and once with the Detroit Red Wings, in 1939.

42) Who was the last regular position player to play goal in an NHL game and who was the goalie he replaced?

a) On October 6, 1960, Jerry Toppazzini of the Boston Bruins replaced Don Simmons in the last minute of play in a 4-1 loss to Detroit. Simmons had been hurt. This was the first time since February 28, 1941, that this scenario had been played out. In that instance, Andy Branigan of the New York Americans replaced Charlie Raynor in the pipes during the last seven minutes of a 5-4 loss to the Detroit Red Wings. Neither player was scored on. Branigan's defence partner in that game was the above mentioned Charlie Conacher.

43) The war years supplied some of the strangest stories in hockey history. A man of the cloth once played goal for the Boston Bruins. When did it happen?

a) On November 27, 1943, the Bruins were desperate for anyone who could play nets. Bert Gardiner had been injured and they were trying anybody when the call went out for George Abbott, who was a Minister of the Cloth. His one and only game in the NHL was a 7-4 loss to the Toronto Maple Leafs.

44) When was the first time two American-born coaches faced each other in an NHL game?

a) On February 22, 1981, Hartford's Larry Pleau and the New York Rangers' Craig Patrick were the respective coaches in a game won by Hartford 6-5.

45) The oldest rookie to play in NHL history was Connie Madigan with St Louis in 1973. He was 38 years old. Jim Anderson, a 37 year old left

winger, who played seven games with LA in 1968 and four playoff games with them in 1969, is the second oldest. Who was the third oldest and what is his claim to fame?

a) Ross Brooks was still a rookie in the 1973-74 season with the Boston Bruins when he tied an existing NHL record of 14 consecutive wins for a goaltender. He turned 36 in October of 1973. The record was held by Tiny Thompson of the Bruins in 1930 and then, in 1976, was broken by another Bruin goalie, Gilles Gilbert, who had 17 wins in a row. Don Beaupre of Minnesota and Tom Barrasso of Pittsburgh have had 14-game streaks since then.

46) Three players have won the Lady Byng Trophy with no penalty minutes. Who were they and when were they winners?

a) Bill Quackenbush, a defenceman with Detroit, won the trophy in 1949 with zero pim's in sixty games. Runner-up that year was Harry Watson, a winger with the Leafs who also had no penalties. The only two other winners with zero penalties were Bill Mosienko, with Chicago in 1945, and Syl Apps, with the Leafs in 1942.

47) Who was the oldest scoring leader in the history of the NHL?

a) Bill Cook was 36 years old when he led the league in 1933 with fifty points. Gordie Howe was 35 when he won his sixth Art Ross Trophy in 1963 with 86 points.

48) Since expansion, one team has dominated the MVP award at the All-Star games with five selections. What team is it and who were the players?

a) The Pittsburgh Penguins have had five MVP's with Mario Lemieux leading the way with three ('85,'88,'90) , Greg Polis ('73) and Syl Apps Jr ('75) .

49) Who was the first American to play in the NHL?

a) Gerry Geran was a forward with the Montreal Wanderers in 1917-18, the first season of the NHL. He was born in Holyoke, Mass., August 3, 1896, and played in all four games the Wanderers existed until their rink, the Westmount Arena, burned down on January 2, 1918.

50) Which player, who has played at least one game in the NHL, is on record as the lightest player in history?

a) A goaltender, who played one game in 1937-38, by the name of Paul Gauthier weighed in at 125 lbs. He was 5'5" tall. Roy "Shrimp" Worters, a goaltender for twelve seasons in the NHL was the shortest player at 5'3"; however, he weighed 135 lbs. Harry Mummery, a defenceman, was supposedly near 270 lbs during his last season with Hamilton Tigers in 1923.

51) There is a by-law in the NHL rules called the Trushinski by-law. It is by-law number 12:6 and it concerns players who have sight in only one eye. Who was it named after, what NHL player did it affect and what junior player tried to fight it?

a) Frank "Snoozer" Trushinski played for a minor pro team called the Kitchener Greenshirts in the 1920s. After losing sight in one eye, he had the misfortune of another injury, this time to his remaining good eye. He lost most of the sight in it. The NHL was concerned about such an incident happening again, so they passed the by-law forbidding anybody to play without proper eyesight in both eyes. In 1939, a leftwinger with Toronto named George Parsons was injured and lost the sight in one eye. He was forced to retire from the game. Greg Neeld was a forward drafted by Buffalo in 1975 who lost sight in one eye in 1973. He, along with lawyer Roy McMurtry, took on the NHL and the by-law, but to no avail. The rule held and Neeld was ineligible to play.

52) Who was the last person to score in a game prior to the players strike of April 1, 1992, and the first person to score after the strike was over on April 12, 1992.

a) Nevin Markwart of the Calgary Flames scored into an empty net at the 19:36 mark of the third period in a 5-2 win over the Edmonton Oilers in a game played in Calgary. Zdeno Ciger, then of the New Jersey Devils scored at the 1:34 mark of the first period in a game against the Buffalo Sabres the day the schedule resumed.

STATS AND STUFF

This chapter is a cross section of statistics, numbers and names. It will mostly be material that you don't hear about anymore except in some instances when it's an anniversary of the event.

1) Who were the original goal scorers of the six expansion teams in 1967?

a) Los Angeles   –   Brian Kilrea

Minnesota   –   Bill Masterson

St Louis   –   Larry Keenan

Philadelphia   –   Bill Sutherland

Pittsburgh   –   Andy Bathgate

Oakland   –   Kent Douglas.

2) When was the first tie game?

a) February 11, 1922. It was 4-4 between the Ottawa Senators and the Toronto St Pat's.

3) When was the first 0-0 game played?

a) December 17, 1924. The teams were the Ottawa Senators and the Hamilton Tigers. The goaltenders were Clint Benedict and Jake Forbes of Ottawa and Hamilton respectively.

4) Who did the first play-by-play on radio of a Montreal Canadiens game?

a) Arthur Dupont on December 22, 1928. Montreal won the game 5-2 over Chicago.

5) What Oakland Seal (California) recorded the most points in one season?

a) Ted Hampson with 75 in 1969. He also won the Bill Masterson Trophy that year becoming the only Seal to win a award.

6) Who played in the first regular season overtime game since 1942?

a) The Detroit Red Wings and the Winnipeg Jets on October 5, 1983. The score ended up 6-6.

7) What two teams participated in the last regular season overtime prior to 1983?

a) On November 10, 1942, the Rangers beat Chicago in overtime 5-3. Confused? In those days teams played ten minutes of OT regardless of who scored. In this case, it was Lynn Patrick and Bryan Hextall.

8) Who scored the first regular season overtime goal since that time?

a) Bob Bourne of the NY Islanders on October 8, 1983, in a 8-7 victory over Washington.

9) What player captained his team longer than anybody?

a) George Armstrong of the Toronto Maple Leafs, 12 seasons from 1958 to 1969, inclusive. Alex Delvecchio was in his twelfth season in 1973-74, but he shared the duties with six other players.

10) Eddie Johnston was the last goaltender to play every minute of his team's games in 1964. Who was the last goaltender to play in every game in one season, but not necessarily every minute?

a) Roger Crozier of the Detroit Red Wings in 1965 played in every game that season including the playoffs, however, he was pulled in two games for a total of 33 minutes. He was replaced by Carl Wetzel who was an American from Detroit. Wetzel would play a total of 269 minutes in five games for the Minnesota Northstars in 1968.

11) On November 27, 1960, Gordie Howe became the first man to record 1,000 points in regular season play. He picked up an assist. Who scored the goal?

a) The Red Wings beat the Leafs that night 2-0. Howe assisted on a goal by Howie Glover who had a good year, picking up 21 goals.

12) Who is the only NHL player to play one game in his career and score one goal?

a) Rolly Huard of the Toronto Maple Leafs played one game in 1930-31 and scored one goal.

13) Who is the only player to score a goal in the NHL before he scored one in Major Junior hockey?

a) Kris Draper in 1990-91 had a three game trial with the Winnipeg Jets and scored once. He then played for his Junior team, the Ottawa 67's, where he recorded 19 goals in 39 games. Also of note, that season he scored twice in the AHL with Moncton, where he played seven games.

14) Mike Bossy, Wayne Gretzky and Jari Kurri all scored their 500th career goals into an empty net. Who were the goaltenders of record those nights?

a) Mike Bossy   - January 2, 1986 vs Boston   - Doug Keans

   Wayne Gretzky - November 22, 1986 vs Vancouver - Troy Gamble

   Jari Kurri   - October 17, 1992 vs Boston   - Andy Moog.

15) Who played and what was the date when the smallest crowd was in attendance at an NHL game?

a) January 22, 1987, in New Jersey, the Devils played Calgary. 344 people braved blizzard conditions to witness a 7-5 Calgary victory. A club was started soon after called the "344 Club".

16) When was the first time that two goaltenders shared a shutout in regular season play?

a) December 2, 1950, Al Rollins and Turk Broda of Toronto in a 0-0 tie with Chicago. Rollins suffered a bad cut and was replaced by Broda. Chicago's goaltender was Harry Lumley, who suffered a broken nose in the game but stayed in and picked up the shutout as well.

17) The night Gordie Howe passed "Rocket" Richard for career goals with his 545th, Terry Sawchuck picked up shutout number 94, tying him with George Hainsworth for the all time lead. When did he get number 95, number 100 and his final one, number 103?

a) January 18, 1964 (still with Detroit)   2-0 vs Montreal for number 95.

March 4, 1967 (with Toronto)   3-0 vs Chicago for number 100.

February 1, 1970 (with Rangers)   6-0 vs Pittsburgh for number 103

18) On March 14, 1968, Sawchuck recorded his 102nd. What was unusual about it?

a) Sawchuck was with the Los Angeles Kings and the game was scheduled against Philadelphia at the Spectrum. However, their roof had blown off so they were playing some of their "home" games in Quebec City. The game was played there and ended up 0-0. The Flyers' goalie was Bernie Parent who picked up career shutout number five and, six years later, would lead them to their first of two straight Stanley Cups.

19) Buffalo's and Vancouver's first amateur draft picks were Gil Perreault and Dale Tallon. Who were their first expansion picks from the other teams?

a) Buffalo took Tom Webster from Boston and immediately traded him to Detroit for goaltender Roger Crozier. Vancouver took defenceman Gary Doak from Boston as well. He played in Vancouver for one season plus six games before being dealt to the Rangers.

20) What two players have the only fighting majors in All-Star game history?

a) Gordie Howe and Gus Mortson in the 1948 game. The game was won 3-1 by the All-Stars over the defending Stanley Cup champions, the Toronto Maple Leafs.

21) Who was the first US born player to score 200 career goals?

a) Reed Larson accomplished the feat while playing for the Boston Bruins in 1986/87.

22) What three General Managers made the jump to GM from the same position in Junior hockey?

a) Leighton "Hap" Emms from Barrie to Boston in 1966; Wren Blair from Oshawa to Minnesota in 1968; and Russ Farwell from Seattle to Philadelphia in 1991.

23) Bobby Orr has the highest recorded plus/minus. Who has the lowest?

a) Bill Mikkelson of the Washington Capitals in 1974-75 was -82.

24) In 1940-41, Bill Cowley led the league in scoring. There was a five way tie for second. Can you name any of the players?

a) Bryan Hextall and Lynn Patrick of the Rangers, Gord Drillon and Syl Apps of Toronto and Syd Howe of Detroit were all tied at 44 points. Cowley was 18 points ahead at 62.

25) Dale Hawerchuck was the second official rookie to score 100 or more points in a season. When did he record his 100th?

a) March 24, 1982, he scored a goal at the 19:19 mark of the third period to help his team, the Winnipeg Jets, to a 5-3 win over LA. He finished with 103 points.

26) When did Bobby Orr score his first regular season goal in the NHL?

a) October 23, 1966, in a 3-2 loss to Montreal. The goalie was Gump Worsley.

27) Who was the first referee to officiate 1,000 games in the NHL?

a) Bruce Hood on November 19, 1983.

28) Who was the only player to score fifty goals or more in a season for a team that finished last in the NHL and who was the goaltender he scored his fiftieth on?

a) On March 14, 1984, in a 7-6 loss to Los Angeles, Pittsburgh's Mike Bullard scored number fifty on the season against goaltender Markus Mattsson.

29) When was the first game postponed in NHL history?

a) January 21, 1936. A game between the Montreal Canadiens and the Toronto Maple Leafs was postponed out of respect for the death of King George V.

30) The Boston Gardens, which is due for closure after the 1994-95 season, was first opened on November 20, 1928. The crowd size can only be estimated for that night because they broke the doors down getting in. The Bruins were beaten that night by the Canadiens 1-0. Who scored the first goal in Boston Gardens?

a) Sylvio Mantha, the captain of the Habs at the time, scored the historic goal.

31) Who was wearing number 10, the night Alex Delvecchio's sweater was retired by the Detroit Red Wings? What number did he switch to?

a) Jimmy Carson and he switched to number 12, in the same fashion as Ray Bourque, who switched to 77, when he presented number 7 to Phil Esposito at centre ice the night the Bruins officially retired that number.

32) Where did the Detroit Cougars, the forerunner to the Falcons and eventually the Red Wings, play their home games their first season in the NHL, 1926-27?

a) They played all their home games in Windsor, Ontario, at the Border City Arena until the Olympia was built.

33) 1929 was known as the year of the shutout. George Hainsworth led the way with 22 in a 44 game schedule. Yet, he didn't win all 22 games and another goalie was voted league MVP. Explain the circumstances.

a) Hainsworth tied one game 0-0, hence his record of 21-0-1 in those games. He did win 22 overall and lost seven. Roy Worters won the Hart Trophy as league MVP with the New York Americans. His 1.21 average on a second place team was seen as the main reason for their success. Considering their top scorers were Billy Burch, 23rd, and Norm Himes, 42nd overall, that made sense.

34) When was the first four game sweep in the Stanley Cup finals?

a) The best-of-seven finals started in 1939. The first sweep was in 1941, when Boston beat Detroit four straight.

35) Alex Connell of the Ottawa Senators has the all-time shutout record of 460 minutes and 49 seconds set in 1927. Here is the breakdown of that amazing record.

Date	TEAMS	SHUTOUT TIME
January 28	Ottawa 2 Canadiens 1	25.39
January 31	Toronto 0 Ottawa 4	60.00
February 2	Mtl Maroons 0 Ottawa 1	69.20
February 7	Ottawa 0 NY Rangers 0	70.00
February 9	Rangers 0 Ottawa 0	70.00
February 16	Pittsburgh 0 Ottawa 0	70.00
February 18	Mtl Canadiens 0 Ottawa 1	60.00
February 22	Ottawa 3 Chicago 2	35.50

Duke Keats of Chicago broke the string at the 15:50 mark of the second period. Of note, the overtime rule was a sudden death or ten minute maximum at that time. In 1928-29 they went to a ten minute overtime period with no sudden death.

36) What is the highest plus/minus ever recorded in one game?

a) Theoren Fleury of the Calgary Flames on February 10, 1993, was +9 in a 13-1 victory over San Jose Sharks. Goaltender Jeff Reese picked up three assists for a record as well.

37) Who scored the 100,000th goal in NHL history?

a) Wilf Paiement, of the Toronto Maple Leafs, on October 12, 1980, scored into an empty net against Philadelphia for the historic marker.

38) When was the first time that two brothers opposed themselves in coaching in the NHL?

   a) December 16, 1934, the Patricks, Frank and Lester, were the first. Frank was at the helm of the Bruins as they beat Lester's Rangers 2-1.

39) What two Montreal Canadien rookies led their team in scoring in 1941?

   a) Johnny Quilty, who would win the Calder Trophy that year, and Joe Benoit, who was the right winger before "Rocket" Richard on the Punch Line with Toe Blake and Elmer Lach. They had 34 and 32 points respectively.

40) The original Mr Zero, Frankie Brimsek, was replaced in the Boston nets in 1949-50, by a rookie out of McGill University who went on to win the Calder Trophy. Who was he?

   a) Jack Gelineau, who would play only two full seasons in the NHL and parts of two others.

41) Who scored the first Red Wing goal in the Joe Louis Arena?

   a) On December 27, 1979, Dennis Sobchuck scored for the Wings in a 3-2 loss to St Louis. The goal was assisted by Mike Foligno.

42) Which defenceman has the record for the fastest three goals in one game?

   a) Denis Potvin, on October 14, 1978, scored three against the Leafs in 3:21, exactly three minutes longer than Bill Mosienko's record of three in 21 seconds.

43) What famous defence combination of the early 1960s shared the same birthday?

   a) Pierre Pilote and Elmer "Moose" Vasko of the Chicago Black Hawks were both born on December 11; Pilote in 1931 and Vasko in 1935. They were partners on defence when Chicago won their last Stanley Cup in 1961.

44) What do the following four players all have in common: Ralph Bowman, Phil Hoene, Ilkka Sinisalo and Reggie Savage?

a) They all scored their first career goals on penalty shots. Bowman in 1934, with the St Louis Eagles; Hoene in 1973, with the LA Kings; Sinisalo in 1981, with the Penguins; and Savage in 1992, with the Washington Capitals.

45) Here are some of the most obscure nickname lines from each decade.

1920s	The A line	NY Rangers
	Frank Boucher Bill Cook	Bun Cook
1930s	The Bread Line	NY Rangers
	Alex Shibicky Neil Colville	Mac Colville
1940s	The Atomic Line	NY Rangers
	Cal Gardener Rene Trudel	Church Russell
1950s	The Rock Line	Toronto
	Gerry James Duke Edmondson	Johnny Wilson
1960s	The Scooter Line	Chicago (second version)
	Stan Mikita Ken Wharren	Doug Mohns
1970s The LILCO (Long Island Lighting Co) Line		NY Islanders
	Bryan Trottier Clark Gillies	Billy Harris
1980s	The Green Beret Line	St. Louis
	Bob Bassen Rich Sutter	Dave Lowrey

The "A" line of the 1920 NY Rangers: Bill Cook, Frank Boucher and Fred "Bun" Cook

46) When was the one and only 0-0 penalty free game, how long did it take to play and who were the goaltenders?

  a) February 20, 1944, was the date of this hockey oddity. The teams were the Chicago Black Hawks and the Toronto Maple Leafs. The game took one hour 55 minutes to play and was officiated by Bill Chadwick. The goaltenders were Paul Bibeault of Toronto and Mike Karakas of Chicago.

47) Which player, who has scored fifty or more goals in a season, has the biggest discrepancy between his top two goal scoring seasons in his career? (Hint - obviously we are dealing with a player who has only one 50 goal season)

a) Jacques Richard had a year in 1982 that he will certainly never forget. After several previous seasons, in which he never exceeded 27 goals, he popped a total of 52 for a difference of 25 from his top season to his second best. Two years after his big season, he was out of the game.

48) Gordie Howe was the oldest player to play in the NHL. Who is the youngest and what was the name of the line he was on?

a) Armand "Bep" Guidolin began in the NHL as a 16 year old in November of 1942 with Boston. He played on a line with Don Gallinger, who was seventeen, and Bill Shill who was nineteen. The Bruins had a popular line at the time called the "Kraut Line"; Milt Schmidt, Woody Dumart and Bobby Bauer. Playing off that name, the media called Guidolin and his linemates the "Sprout Line".

49) Who was the first Russian trained hockey player to score a goal in the NHL and when was it?

a) On October 17, 1982, Victor Nechaev, while playing for the Los Angeles Kings, scored a goal against the Rangers. It was the only goal he scored in a three game trial with the Kings. He was 27 years old.

50) Mike Gartner has the unusual distinction of scoring his 100th, 200th and 300th career goals against the same goaltender. Who was it?

a) Gartner scored all three of those goals against Glen Hanlon. His 100th was scored in 1982; Hanlon was with Vancouver. His 200th was scored in 1984; Hanlon was with the Rangers. His 300th was scored in 1987; Hanlon was with Detroit. Mike Gartner was also the first man to score his 500th goal, 500th assist, 1,000th point and play his 1,000th game all in the same season 1991-92.

51) The Vancouver Canucks' first regular season shutout was a 0-0 game against Toronto. When was it and who were the goaltenders?

a) On October 27, 1971, the Canucks picked up their first official shutout. Dunc Wilson was the goalie on record for the Canucks; Bernie Parent had the shutout for the Leafs.

TEAM TRIVIA

The final chapter of this book will include one question pertaining to each team currently in the NHL. It will be an oddity concerning a player or the team itself and it will be something that you quite likely have never heard of, or by now, have certainly forgotten.

1) Who scored the very first goal in Boston Bruin history? (This is not to be confused with the question earlier in the book regarding the first goal in the Boston Gardens.)

a)Carson Cooper scored the first Boston Bruin goal on December 1, 1924, as they beat the Montreal Maroons 2-1.

2) Three individuals on the Buffalo Sabres created hockey history in 1992. Who were they and what did they do?

a)For the first time in NHL history, three players on one team accumulated 300 or more penalty minutes in one season. Rob Ray had 354, Gord Donnelly had 316 (although 11 of those minutes were picked up with Winnipeg), and Brad May had 309 minutes.

3) The Flames organization (including Atlanta) have only been involved in one scoreless tie in their history. When was it and who were the goaltenders?

a)On November 7, 1976, the Atlanta Flames and the Detroit Red Wings played to a 0-0 draw. Phil Myre was in the pipes for the Flames, Eddie Giacomin for the Wings.

4) In 1976, Bobby Orr signed as a free agent with Chicago. Because of knee problems, he played only 26 games with the Hawks before retiring in 1979. Who wore number 4 for Chicago before Bobby Orr and who wore it after him?

a)Dave Logan wore it until Orr's arrival; Keith Brown took it a full season after Orr had retired.

5)What Detroit Red Wing has the distinction of being the youngest player to play in an NHL All-Star game?

a)Steve Yzerman was 18 years and nine months old when he played in the 1984 All-Star game.

6)What five Edmonton Oilers scored the five Stanley Cup winning goals in their history?

a)Ken Linsmen 1984, second period versus the Islanders; Paul Coffey 1985, first period versus the Flyers; Jari Kurri 1987, second period versus the Flyers; Wayne Gretzky 1988, second period versus the Bruins; and Craig Simpson 1990, second period versus the Bruins.

7)The Hartford Whalers' first home victory in the NHL has an asterisk beside it. Why, and who scored the winning goal?

a)The date was October 19, 1979, and Hartford beat Los Angeles 6-3. The winning goal was scored by Mark Howe. The game was actually played in Springfield, home to the Whalers for two years, after the roof at the Civic Center had collapsed in 1978 under the weight of snow and ice.

8)The first ever playoff overtime goal scored against the Los Angeles Kings was scored by a player who was on the 1967 Stanley Cup winning Toronto Maple Leafs. Who was he?

a)Milan Marcetta played three games with the Leafs in 1967, picking up no points, but he did get his name on the Cup. The following year, he was with the Minnesota North Stars when they eliminated the Los Angeles Kings in the quarter-finals. Marcetta scored in overtime in Game Six to force a Game Seven which Minnesota won 9-4.

9) Who scored the first goal in the Dallas Stars' regular season opener?

a) On October 5, 1993, the Stars beat Detroit 6-4 in the first game played at the Reunion Arena and the first game in Dallas' history. Neal Broten scored at the 3:51 mark of the first period with an assist going to Mike McPhee.

10) What year did the Montreal Canadiens finish with a record under .500 and make the Stanley Cup finals?

a) They were close in 1984. They were five games under .500 and came within two wins of a berth in the finals. However, in 1951, they made the finals after another season of five games under .500. Their record was 25-30-15 and they were beaten by the Leafs on Bill Barilko's goal in overtime in Game Five.

11) What two goaltenders shared the first shutout in New Jersey Devil history?

a) On December 4, 1983, the Devils shutout the Detroit Red Wings 6-0. The goose egg was shared by Ron Low, who played 21 minutes of the game, and Glen "Chico" Resch, who played 39 minutes of the game.

12) How many New York Islanders were on both the very first Islander team in the NHL and the first Islander team that won the Stanley Cup?

a) Four players who played in that first season were there eight seasons later when they won the Cup. Goaltender Billy Smith, forwards Lorne Henning, Bobby Nystrom and Gary Howatt.

13) Hall of Fame goaltender Harry Lumley played for five of the "original six" teams in the NHL. Which was the only team he did not play for and what team did he play only twenty minutes for?

a) Lumley, who was nicknamed "Apple Cheeks", never played for the Montreal Canadiens and, during the 1943-44 season, he played twenty minutes for the Rangers, but never again. The unique situation happened on December 22, 1943, when he was a 17 year old back-up goaltender for the Red Wings. In a game against the Rangers, regular goalie Ken McAuley went down with an injury in the third period. Lumley had been called up the previous game by Detroit because regular goalie Normie Smith had been beaten for seven goals in a blowout loss to Chicago. Smith, however, played against the Rangers, so Detroit let the young Lumley suit up for the Rangers. He allowed no goals in the 5-3 Detroit victory.

14) There's only been one player in NHL history to sign as a free agent as an 18 year old, and play at least one game that season. Coincidentally, the same player also scored the first shorthanded goal in the modern Ottawa Senators' history. Who is he?

a) Mark Freer was signed as a free agent by the Philadelphia Flyers in 1986 and played one game for them that season, picking up an assist. He played the rest of the year with his junior team, the Peterborough Petes. After being claimed on waivers by Ottawa, he was part of history for the Senators when he scored their first shorthanded goal in the modern era on December 26, 1992, in Quebec against goaltender Ron Hextall.

15) The first time the Montreal Canadiens lost to an expansion team at the Forum was November 4, 1967. The opposition was the Philadelphia Flyers who won the game 4-1. Who scored the Flyer hat-trick that night?

a) It was the first hat-trick in Flyer history and it was scored by a Quebec native and a man who won a Stanley Cup ring with the Habs in 1966. He name was Leon Rochefort. Ironically, he would pick up another Stanley Cup victory with the Canadiens in 1971.

16) The first penalty shot goal in Pittsburgh Penguin history was scored by a native of Flin Flon, Manitoba. Who was he and when was it?

a) The date was January 31, 1968. The location was the St Louis Arena and the goaltender was Glenn Hall. Twenty-nine year old George Konick gained Pittsburgh immortality by scoring on a penalty shot. It was the only season he played in the NHL.

17) The first hat-trick scored by a member of the Quebec Nordiques in the NHL was on October 10, 1979, their first game in their new league. The player who did it, is one of only two rookies to score a hat-trick in their first game. Who was it and whose record did he tie?

a) Real Cloutier scored all three Quebec goals in a 5-3 loss to Atlanta. Cloutier tied a record first set on January 14, 1943 (by Alex Smart of the Montreal Canadiens), as he scored three goals in a 5-1 Montreal victory over Chicago.

18) When did Brett Hull score the first empty net goal of his NHL career?

a) Avowing at one time never to score into an empty net, Hull finally did on January 13, 1994. It was against the Edmonton Oilers and it was the sixth goal in a 6-4 St Louis win. By the way, it was the 386th goal of his career, not including playoffs.

19) The San Jose Sharks played their home games in the San Francisco Cow Palace their first two seasons in the league. How did the Cow Palace get its name and what was its original name?

a) During construction of the building in the 1930s, a San Francisco newspaper columnist dubbed the sight a "palace for cows". The nickname held up. However, it wasn't until the 1950s that "Cow Palace" was painted on the exterior of the building and it was 1963 before the Directors of the building changed the legal name to Cow Palace from First National Livestock Exposition and Rodeo.

20) Two players of the Tampa Bay Lightnings' opening game roster had fathers who played in the NHL. Who were the players and their fathers?

a) Adam Creighton, who was in the starting lineup against Chicago on October 7, 1992, and Ken Hodge Jr who scored the game winning goal against Chicago on the same night, both had fathers in the NHL. Ironically, both their dads played for the Black Hawks at one time in their careers. Their names were Dave Creighton and Ken Hodge Sr.

21) The Toronto Maple Leafs changed their name from Toronto St Patrick's on February 14, 1927. That season (1926-27), a 19 year old centre began his pro career with Toronto. Forty-eight years later he was inducted into the Hockey Hall of Fame. Who was he and what were some of his accomplishments?

a) Carl Voss was the man's name. His career as a player was unusual to say the least. To begin with, his mother had to sign his first contract with Toronto in 1926, because he was under 21 years of age. Unfortunately, his mother's signature didn't guarantee a spot in the lineup and he only played a total of 14 games for Toronto, spending most of his time in the minors. It was 6 years later, in 1932, when he finally cracked the NHL fulltime; first with the NY Rangers then Detroit. It was in that season that the Chelsea, Mass native became the inaugural winner of the Rookie Of The Year award which, four years later, became known as the Calder Trophy. He played for a total of eight teams in his 261 game career, including a Stanley Cup winner in 1938 with Chicago. He finished his playing career after that season and went on to become Referee-in-Chief of the NHL for many years until replaced by Scotty Morrison.

22) The first playoff, game-winning goal scored by a Vancouver Canuck in their history was against the Montreal Canadiens in 1975. The goal scorer was an original Montreal draft pick. Who was he?

a) Garry Monahan scored the second goal in a 2-1 Vancouver victory. He was originally drafted by the Habs in 1963, but only played 14 games with them in 1968 and 1969 before being dealt to Detroit for Peter Mahovlich. That series in 1975 was eventually won by the Canadiens four games to one, with the series winner being scored in overtime by Guy Lafleur. It was the first playoff overtime goal against the Canucks and it was Lafleur's first overtime goal in his career.

23)The Washington Capitals have played 1,616 games in the regular season and playoffs between their inception in 1974 and the end of the 1992-93 regular season. One man has seen every game. Who is he?

a)Ron Weber, their veteran radio broadcaster, began his career as the voice of the Baltimore Clippers and joined the Capitals for their first season in 1974. He is also a past president of the NHL Broadcasters Association.

24)The 1980-81 Winnipeg Jets roster featured four future coaches in the NHL. Who are they?

a)Rick Bowness, Barry Long, Rick Dudley and Barry Melrose all suited up that season for the Jets. Bowness and Melrose were both coaching in the 1993-94 season. Long was a runner-up for the Jack Adams Award for Coach of the Year in 1985. He was at the helm of the Jets and lost to Mike Keenan, who was running the Flyers at that time. Rick Dudley was head coach of the Sabres from 1989/90 into 1992.

25)Who scored the first regular season goals for both Anaheim and Florida?

a)Scott Mellanby scored the first goal for the Florida Panthers in a 4-4 tie with the Chicago Black Hawks on October 6, 1993. Sean Hill did the trick for the Anaheim Mighty Ducks on October 8, 1993, in a 7-2 loss to Detroit.

ABOUT THE AUTHOR

By the time Liam Maguire was ten, he had accumulated and stored a vast supply of hockey data. At the age of sixteen, the passion turned into an obsession of studying, memorizing, reading and researching even the smallest hockey trivia detail.

The crowning glory of his youth took place in 1981 when he was invited as a guest on the Hal Anthony Talk Show on CFRA Radio in Ottawa. His destiny was, at that point, assured and he became the unofficial hockey trivia expert.

His public appearances number over 500, having met many hockey personalities, players, media and fans - as he constantly adds to his cache of information. Liam doesn't give you just the straight answer to the question, but adds the ultimate "and did you know . . . " to each query.

While Liam enjoys playing hockey in a local men's league, his real hobby is precisely answering everything and anything about NHL hockey.

He is engaged to be married and, of course, proposed at centre ice at the Montreal Forum.

For more copies of
LIAM MAGUIRE'S Hockey Trivia Book 1
send $9.95 plus $3.00 shipping and handling to:
GENERAL STORE PUBLISHING HOUSE
1 Main Street, Burnstown, Ontario
Canada, K0J 1G0

(613) 432-7697 0r 1-800-465-6072
Fax: (613) 432-7184

OTHER SPORTS BOOKS BY GSPH

White Gold	$14.95
Killer	$14.95
The Ottawa Sports Book	$29.95
The Renfrew Millionaires	$14.95
Line Drive	$12.95
Not Bad, Eh?	$19.95
Level Ice	$ 6.95

For each copy, include $3.00 to cover shipping, handling, and GST.
Make cheque or money order payable to:
GENERAL STORE PUBLISHING HOUSE
1 Main Street, Burnstown, Ontario
Canada, K0J 1G0